THE **WHARNCLIFFE C**

IPSWICH

Bob Malster

A map of Ipswich town centre produced by W.S. Cowell's in the 1920s.

THE **WHARNCLIFFE COMPANION** TO

IPSWICH

AN **A** TO **Z** OF LOCAL HISTORY

ROBERT MALSTER

Wharncliffe Books

In memory of
Bernard Barrell
who contributed so
much to this book

First published in Great Britain in 2005 by
Wharncliffe Books
an imprint of
Pen & Sword Books Ltd
47 Church Street
Barnsley
South Yorkshire
S70 2AS

ISBN 1-903425-69-7

A CIP catalogue record for this book is
available from the British Library

Typeset in 10/11.5pt Plantin by Mac Style Ltd, Scarborough, N. Yorkshire
Printed and bound in England by CPI UK

Pen & Sword Books Ltd incorporates the Imprints of Pen & Sword Aviation,
Pen & Sword Maritime, Pen & Sword Military, Wharncliffe Local History,
Pen & Sword Select, Pen and Sword Military Classics and Leo Cooper.

For a complete list of Wharncliffe titles, please contact
Wharncliffe Books Limited
47 Church Street, Barnsley, South Yorkshire, S70 2AS, England
E-mail: enquiries@pen-and-sword.co.uk
Website: www.wharncliffebooks.co.uk

Contents

Acknowledgements

It is now more than sixty years since I came as a small boy to Ipswich on an excursion train hauled by Patrick Stirling's Great Northern Railway No. 1, brought out of retirement in York railway museum to celebrate the jubilee of the Flying Scotsman. Even then Ipswich had a fascination for me, though then it was largely because of a shop in Friars Street that had a model railway in the window.

Since then my interest in the town's history has widened far beyond railways, full-size or small-scale. It was first encouraged by Harry Wilton, who probably knew more about Ipswich and Suffolk than anyone else in the days just after the Second World War and was always willing to share his knowledge with others. It was from him that I first heard the saying that 'Now I'm retired I'm so busy I don't know how I ever found time to go to work!'

There have been others who have helped me on my way since, including the many who have given me the postcards and photographs with which this book is illustrated; I cannot name them all, but to every one of them I give my thanks. John Fairclough has proved a source of both friendship and wise counsel as we have probed together into the murky history of the town, and Dr John Blatchly has been an ever-ready source of information.

To them and to others too numerous to mention I offer my thanks. I also owe a deep debt of gratitude to my editor, Gerard Hill, who has saved me from the results of many a mistake; if any still remain, the responsibility for them is mine alone.

Robert Malster
Ipswich 2004

Introduction

Although Ipswich is not to be found in lists of popular historic towns and is not visited by swarms of tourists in the way that York and Canterbury are, it can claim to be one of the most historic towns in Britain. Established in the seventh century AD, it is the earliest post-Roman urban settlement in England, with a history of continuous settlement of more than 1400 years.

It is thought that the Wuffinga kings, whose burial ground is at Sutton Hoo, established the settlement of Gippeswyk as a trading centre for their kingdom. Evidence of trade in Saxon times has come to light in the shape of amphorae, in which wine was imported, and fragments of millstone, both from the Rhineland. Much wider links stretching as far as Constantinople might be inferred from the fabulous contents of the burial ship excavated at Sutton Hoo which indicate that the kingdom was carrying on trade with all parts of the then-known world.

That was not the beginning of Ipswich's story, however. There is considerable evidence of Roman occupation in the area occupied by the modern town, and from Belstead has come a hoard of gold torcs to show that there were wealthy Iron Age peoples living in the Ipswich area in the first century BC.

By the time Ipswich received its charter from King John, giving the townspeople the right to elect their own local officers and a considerable measure of self-government, it already had some six hundred years of urban history behind it. Archaeologists have discovered Saxon kilns producing the first post-Roman wheel-thrown pottery, named by them Ipswich ware, which was distributed widely along the east coast of England. The unsettled times when Vikings or Danes were raiding eastern England (they 'harried' Ipswich in 991) do not appear to have led to any lasting decline in the importance of the town; indeed, the first town bank and ditch seems to have been made by the Danes during their occupation.

In the Middle Ages its merchants traded first in wool and then in woollen cloth, which was exported through the port of Orwell downriver; they sent their ships to Bordeaux for wine and to Iceland for dried fish; and they enriched the town by their benefactions. While Ipswich had its weavers and other textile workers operating within the town, much of what was exported over the town's quays came from other centres of the woollen trade in south Suffolk and adjoining areas of Essex.

Shipbuilding on the banks of the Orwell was important at least from the thirteenth century when Ipswich provided a galley and its attendant barge for King Edward I. In the seventeenth century the town gained the nickname of 'the Shipyard of London' because of the number of ships built for influential

London merchants, who might have been expected to favour builders on the Thames. In the nineteenth century Ipswich shipbuilders were launching large ships for the trade with India.

With the Industrial Revolution, the Ransomes built up an engineering business based at first on the demands of the agricultural community. What began as a general ironfounding business in 1789 grew in the following century into an enterprise that played a major part in the development of agricultural machinery, especially ploughs. It also diversified into civil engineering, building a new Stoke Bridge in 1818–19, and railway engineering, besides developing an overseas trade that put it in the forefront of Victorian enterprise. The breadth of its influence is illustrated by the fact that the original firm supplied ploughs, steam engines and thrashing machines to almost the entire developing world and an offshoot company built the first railway in China, staffed by men from Ipswich.

The town's prosperity in Victorian times and since has meant that many relics of its more distant past have been swept away, as streets have been widened and new buildings erected in the town centre. In the nineteenth century there was a wave of nostalgia for what was being lost that resulted in photographers such as William Vick generating a thriving trade in photographs of those buildings that were being swept away. Such was the demand for his pictures of old Ipswich that Vick had to make copies of his glass negatives in order to facilitate the production of prints; his copy negatives are to be seen among the collection of his work in the Suffolk Record Office in Gatacre Road, Ipswich. The pictures that Vick printed in his studio at Barrack Corner happily remain as a record of a delightful old town that disappeared in the name of progress; many of his photographs illustrate this book.

While small towns like Lavenham retained their old houses and public buildings because of their relative poverty after the loss of the woollen trade, Ipswich on a wave of new-found prosperity cleared away many of its medieval buildings, including the original town hall, once St Mildred's Church. The tourists flock to Lavenham, but they are not tempted in the same numbers to Ipswich and its rich but somewhat dispersed heritage.

It has been said that Ipswich has a greater wealth of timber-framed buildings even than the historic area of the city of York, but they have to be sought out. The Ancient House in the Buttermarket and Christchurch Mansion are the jewels in Ipswich's crown, but there remain also the lovely timber-framed building once known as the Wolsey Pharmacy on the corner of Silent Street and other timber-framed buildings nearby in St Peter's Street. In Fore Street there survive the fabulous Isaac Lord complex and the Old Neptune Inn, both of them of sufficient interest and value to attract the discerning visitor and to impart a glow of pride to the native.

Sad though it is that the Old Coffee House has gone from Tavern Street, that one of the country's oldest school buildings, Felaw's House, was lost to slum clearance in the 1960s, and that the Friends' Meeting Houses were demolished more recently, leaving a wasteland in which Robert Ransome's grave remains unmarked, Ipswich still retains wonderful reminders of its long and interesting past. Thanks to the work of the Ipswich Building Preservation Trust and the Historic Churches Trust, both backed by the Borough Council, a great deal is being done to prevent more of the town's heritage from sliding into dereliction. It is hoped that the preservation trust will soon be able to restore the one-time Wolsey Pharmacy, at present boarded up; meanwhile, volunteers are opening certain of the redundant town churches to visitors during the summer.

So much more could be done to enable Ipswich to take its rightful place among Britain's historic towns if only there were no underlying denial of its special part in the country's story. Perhaps this book, to which so many people have willingly contributed the results of their researches, will help to persuade the unbelievers that Ipswich is an historic town.

★   ★   ★

There is so much of interest in Ipswich now as well as in the past that it has been difficult to choose items for this book. It would have been possible to write much more, on many more subjects, had there been space.

Nonetheless, it is hoped that this book will serve to show what an interesting town Ipswich is. Perhaps it will also provide the answer to some of those arguments that develop among Ipswichians about the town's recent past. If the argument tends to show that the author has got it wrong, he can only apologise and say that he did his best.

The Wharncliffe Companion to Ipswich

AIRCRAFT MANUFACTURE

During the First World War a number of engineering companies and others were asked to build aircraft for the Royal Flying Corps. Among them were Ransomes, Sims & Jefferies and another Ipswich firm, Frederick Tibenham, whose works were in Turret Lane, not far from the Old Cattle Market. Ransomes erected hangars in a former brickyard claypit on the north side of Fore Hamlet and built large numbers of FE2b fighters – useful pusher biplanes developed by the Royal Aircraft Factory at Farnborough before the war but not brought into service until 1915 – and then 400 Airco DH6, one of Geoffrey de Havilland's early designs. With an engine that was never powerful enough, the DH6 acquired an unsavoury reputation and was known by pilots as 'the widow-maker'. Ransomes built 790 aircraft, and they would have built more; they received an order for the Vickers Vimy twin-engined biplane bomber, but the order was cancelled at the end of the war.

Employees of Ransomes, Sims & Jefferies, many of them women, lined up in front of an FE2b in one of the hangars in Fore Hamlet, known to generations of Ransomes workers as the White City.

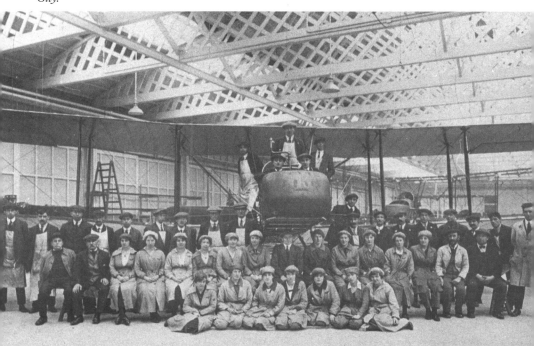

Tibenham's, a woodworking firm, built wings and other parts for the FE2b and also propellers, which were sent away to other aircraft manufacturers. No doubt with a view to boosting morale among the Ipswich workers, Ransomes was sent a letter in 1917 stating that B401, the first FE2b turned out by the company, had been involved in shooting down the Zeppelin L48 at Theberton on 17 June that year, but subsequent research has thrown doubt on the claim. Unlike some engineering concerns such as Boulton & Paul of Norwich, which continued to produce aircraft after the war, Ransomes left that business; the 'White City' works, as it became known to the employees, was turned over to the production of lawnmowers. The hangars have now been demolished and other buildings have taken their place.
☞ *See also Ransomes, Sims & Jefferies*

AIRPORT

Opened in 1930 by the Prince of Wales, the Ipswich Municipal Aerodrome was a far-sighted attempt to place the town firmly on the map 'as an essential link in the chain of aerial communications,' as the corporation put it. When he landed in his personal Westland Wapiti, Prince Edward (later, briefly, King Edward VIII and then after his abdication Duke of Windsor) was welcomed by Mr A.L. Clouting, the first Labour Mayor of Ipswich.

The Municipal Aerodrome in time expanded to become Ipswich Airport, but the early dreams of attracting major airlines such as KLM and Lufthansa did not materialise, though in 1935 it was possible to fly (on Sundays only) to Southend and Ramsgate in a De Havilland DH84 Dragon operated by Crilly Airways. After being run by Suffolk Aero Club on the corporation's behalf for some years, the airport became the responsibility of the Whitney Straight Corporation, which opened new terminal buildings in 1938 and operated a daily service to Clacton-on-Sea using a five-seater Short Scion.

The Royal Air Force moved in as soon as the Second World War broke out and the airport became a satellite of RAF Wattisham, a bomber station some twelve miles to the west. Bristol Blenheim bombers of 110 Squadron, based at Wattisham, flew from Ipswich on the first British air raid of the war, attacking German warships at their anchorage. Later in the war Ipswich became a fighter station, and was also home to target-towing aircraft which operated with the army's anti-aircraft batteries in the region.

When peace returned, Ipswich Airport resumed its civilian role, but hampered by a lack of customs facilities. Channel Airways flew services from Ipswich to the Continent, but aircraft had to land at Southend to obtain customs clearance on the way. Club flying also resumed, and at one time the airport was home to some interesting veteran aircraft as well as modern light planes.

Continuing the royal connection begun by the Prince of Wales, Queen Elizabeth II and the Duke of Edinburgh flew to the airport in an aircraft of the Queen's Flight at the beginning of her jubilee visit to Ipswich in 1977. The airport had only grass runways in an era when the increasing weight and size of airliners was demanding concrete runways and taxiways. Eventually, in 1988, Suckling Airways moved the last commercial service elsewhere.

Faced with a need for land for housing, Ipswich Borough Council decided to use the site for that. The airport closed in December 1996 and in 2004 building operations were going on where for 70 years flying activities had been predominant.

☞ *See also Clouting, Arthur*

ALEXANDER, RICHARD DYKES

The son of Dykes Alexander, a Quaker banker from Needham Market who was much involved in Ipswich business affairs, R.D. Alexander was born on 15 August 1788. He became a partner in the family firm of Alexander and Company, whose 'Yellow Bank' stood in Bank Street, which formerly ran between the bottom of Foundation Street and Key Street; it was known as the 'Yellow Bank' because of the partners' reforming sympathies and to differentiate it from the Cobbolds' 'Blue Bank'. Retiring from business at the age of forty, R.D. Alexander devoted himself to public work and to his hobby: he was a pioneer of amateur photography. Some of his photographs were acquired by Suffolk Record Office in 1978 at Sotheby's Belgravia. Among them were pictures of the Ipswich Ragged School, an institution that received much support from him. He was also involved in the temperance movement, and built the Temperance Hall at the corner of High Street and Crown Street in 1840 at his own expense; it later became an iron foundry.

☞ *See also Ragged School; Temperance Hall*

ALEXANDRA PARK

Between Suffolk College and Grove Lane is one of the open spaces which Ipswich is fortunate to have. Named after Queen Alexandra, the wife of King Edward VII, this 11-acre piece of land was acquired by the corporation in 1903 for £6,544 when the Hill House estate was sold by auction at the Great White Horse Hotel on the death of Mrs Ann Byles, widow of Jeremiah Byles. Hill House, for more than a century the home of the Byles family, was demolished and most of the estate was developed for housing by the Ipswich Freehold Land Society, the Ipswich Permanent Benefit Building Society and others. On a drinking fountain in the park is an inscription 'in remembrance of the Byles family to whom this park belonged for more than 100 years, this drinking fountain was erected in 1905 by Charles Henry Cowell, Alderman of the Borough and twice Mayor of Ipswich, whose mother was Marianne Byles, born at Hill House, 1801'.

4 The Wharncliffe Companion to Ipswich

ALLENBY, VISCOUNT
Although he was not born in Suffolk, the fact that soon after his birth his parents purchased Felixstowe House as their summer home gave Field Marshal Edmund Allenby a close connection with the county that was taken full advantage of when he returned home after the First World War. He established a sound reputation as a soldier during the South African War, and he built on this very considerably as commander of the Egyptian Expeditionary Force from June 1917. Never one to lead from the rear, he moved his general headquarters to the Palestine border, close to the front, planning to clear the Turks from Palestine and Syria. It was the last great campaign in which cavalry were employed in strategic mass; the Suffolk Yeomanry marched 550 miles in just thirty-eight days, fighting four considerable actions during that advance. He received the honorary freedom of Ipswich on 6 October 1919.
☛ *See also Freemen*

ALNESBOURNE
North of the Orwell between Ipswich and Nacton stood Alnesbourne Priory in the parish of St Felix Hallowtree. According to Domesday Book Alnesbourne was before 1066 held by the Cathedral Priory of St Andrew at Rochester, which also established a subordinate priory of St Felix at Walton, not many miles away. The church of Alnesbourne Priory was dedicated to St Mary, but interestingly that of Hallowtree was dedicated (like Walton Priory) to St Felix, who in the seventh century came from Kent, and brought teachers from Rochester, apparently giving his name to Felixstowe. The name and site of the priory survived as a farm, and in the early twentieth century there was an Alnesbourne Priory Dairy that delivered milk in Ipswich. The name Hallowtree ('Holy Tree') still survives as that of a Scout camp site, now just on the eastern side of the Ipswich by-pass.

AMERICA
A hotbed of Puritanism, Ipswich contributed quite largely to the wave of emigration created by the actions of the High Church party in the early seventeenth century. In 1611 the corporation 'adventured' £100 towards the cost of ships to carry settlers to Virginia, where the Virginia Company had founded the port of Jamestown in 1607. When in 1620 the Pilgrim Fathers sailed in the *Mayflower*, some of the emigrants were from Suffolk, and within a few years they were followed by many others, some of whom sailed from Ipswich. The *Mayflower* may well have been built in Ipswich, for she was described as 'of Harwich' in 1609 and her captain, Christopher Jones, was a Harwich man. In 1630 the Winthrop Fleet, eleven ships carrying almost 700 passengers, sailed with members of the Winthrop family of Groton and

others from Suffolk and north Essex heading for a new life across the Atlantic. One of the settlements founded by the Winthrop Fleet was named Ipswich 'in acknowledgement of the great honour and kindness done to our people who took shipping there'.

The bishop's commissary for the Archdeaconry of Suffolk, Henry Dade, complained to Archbishop Laud in 1634 about the increasing emigration of people disaffected to the government of the Church of England. His complaints led to the Privy Council preventing the departure of two vessels from Ipswich early in March that year for New England with 80 emigrants in each. Perhaps this only delayed their departure, for the *Elizabeth* and the *Francis*, both of Ipswich, sailed down the Orwell 'bound for New England the last of Aprill'.

One of the larger ships sailing across the Atlantic was the 400-ton *Great Hope* of Ipswich, which arrived in America in mid-August 1635, after weathering a storm which had wrecked one ship and nearly wrecked another. Three more ships, the *Mary Anne* of Yarmouth, the *John and Dorothy* of Ipswich and the *Rose* of Yarmouth, arrived on the American coast from Ipswich in June 1637. The following year the *Diligent* of Ipswich was among twenty ships that crossed the Atlantic with at least 3,000 men, women and children.

ANCIENT HOUSE

Of all the town's historic buildings, the Ancient House at the corner of the Buttermarket and St Stephen's Lane is the one that popular opinion regards as worthy of preservation. Perhaps the fact that Robert Sparrowe chose to commemorate the Restoration of the Monarchy by covering the front of his home with elaborate pargeting is responsible for the affection that citizens have for this building. The oldest part of it was already well over a hundred years old when the decorative plasterwork was added to the façade of the new section fronting the Buttermarket, possibly just before the visit of Charles II in 1668.

Besides the Royal Arms, the centrepiece of the display, the pargeting shows the four continents, Europe represented by a crowned female figure, Asia by another female figure sitting under a palm tree, Africa by a naked man sitting on a tree stump under a parasol, and America by a man wearing a feather head-dress and holding arrows in one hand and a tobacco pipe in the other; Australia, of course, had not at that time been discovered. Other panels show the three elements, Earth, Water and Air, and on the western gable is St George, in the garb of a seventeenth-century gentleman, dealing with a recumbent dragon.

The Ancient House has had many owners, one of the more interesting being George Copping, draper and fishmonger, who acquired it in 1567. He it was who had the stained cloths or linen wall-hangings made, one showing Hercules slaying the Hydra and the other showing Hercules' struggle with the

The pargeted front of the Ancient House has created interest among visitors for more than three hundred years. When the design was applied, perhaps to celebrate the Restoration of King Charles II, the Ancient House was a private residence, but in the nineteenth century it became a bookshop and library, as it was when this photograph was taken.

giant Antaeus. The cloths no doubt owe their survival to Copping's instructions to his wife that nothing should be removed from the house after his death, and to the panelling that concealed one of them until restoration work followed the Borough Council's acquisition of the property in 1979.

William Sparrowe took over the house in 1591, and members of his family owned it for close on three hundred years. There is a tradition, unsupported by any firm evidence, that Charles II hid in a secret room in the attics of the Ancient House while on the run after the Battle of Worcester in 1651. There were Royalist sympathisers in the town, but Ipswich was strongly Puritan in sentiment and government and so Charles was unlikely to have sought sanctuary in such a town. Indeed, Robert Sparrowe seems to have concealed his Royalist enthusiasm until after the Restoration in 1660.

During the nineteenth century the Ancient House was occupied by a succession of printers, who at first lived in the house and had their printing presses in premises at the back, in St Stephen's Lane. For well over a century the Ancient House was a bookshop; it is now a domestic utensils shop run by Lakeland Ltd.

☞ *See also Buttermarket*

ANGLESEA ROAD
In earlier days known as Peddars Lane, Anglesea Road may have derived its new name from Sir Henry William Paget, 1st Marquis of Anglesey, who lost a leg at Waterloo. His son, General Lord George Augustus Frederick Paget, led the 4th Light Dragoons in the charge of the Light Brigade at Balaclava, became inspector-general of cavalry in 1871 and possibly had some connection with Ipswich Barracks; there is a Paget Road leading off Anglesea Road.

ARGENTINE, RICHARD
Headmaster of Ipswich Grammar School from 1538 to 1558, Richard Argentine, or Sexton as he was originally known, was a notorious turncoat in an age of religious upheaval. Born in 1511, he came to Ipswich at the age of thirty-six to become usher of the school. Much of what we know of him comes from John Foxe, who gives a colourful account of the schoolmaster's exploits in his *Actes and Monuments*. A married man, Argentine seems to have impressed the Bailiffs of Ipswich, who wrote recommending his promotion from usher to master in 1538. It was doubtless due to the energy and influence of the Protestant headmaster that more than a score of books were published over Ipswich imprints in 1548, three of them translations by Argentine of the works of the Protestant reformers Martin Luther, Bernadino Ochino and Ulrich Zwingli.

When Edward VI was succeeded by his Catholic sister Mary in 1553, Argentine had a sudden switch of conscience. As the new queen, on her way from Framlingham to her proclamation in London, called on Sir Humphrey Wingfield at his mansion in Tacket Street, Argentine made a speedy return to the old religion. To quote Foxe, there was now 'none more hot in papistry and superstition than he'. On the death of his wife a year later Argentine became a priest and was instituted to the livings of St Clement and St Helen in Ipswich. Before long he was also priest of Whitton, and of Brantham with East Bergholt, though there were soon complaints that as pastor at Brantham he was grossly negligent, 'to the great peryll of the inhabitantes'.

With Mary's reign drawing to its end, Argentine realised that Protestant religion would soon be restored. His persecution of Protestants meant he was unpopular, so he resigned the mastership he had held for twenty years and left for London, where he soon 'began to show himself again as a perfect Protestant'.

On his death in 1568 Argentine still held the living of St Helen's at Ipswich, though his absence had clearly prevented him officiating in the Ipswich church for some years. His replacement, a man who had no cause to respect Argentine, refused to name him when reciting the pastoral succession in the parish in a lawsuit in 1586, referring merely to 'another'; it was 'a dignified and understated insult which the former Ipswich schoolmaster richly deserved', as Dr John Blatchly observes.

See John Blatchly, *A Famous Antient Seed-Plot of Learning* (Ipswich School 2003)

☛ *See also Bailiffs; Boy Bishop; Grammar School*

ASSEMBLY ROOMS

The centre of social life in eighteenth-century Ipswich was the Assembly House or Assembly Rooms, where the better classes might meet at the card table or at balls held during the races or to celebrate special occasions such as the king's birthday. In the earlier part of the century, Benjamin Crocker ran the Assembly House in St Peter's Street, opposite the tower of St Peter's Church; a room in his next-door house served as a waiting room for the menservants, who were called thence when needed to accompany their masters and mistresses home. A New Assembly House was opened next to Dod's Coffee House on the corner of Tavern Street and Tower Street on 8 November 1753; more than three hundred gentlemen and ladies attended the opening concert and ball.

The Assembly Rooms and adjacent Coffee House were acquired in 1798 by John Cobbold, of the local brewing family, but it was not long before a new meeting place for the gentry and their ladies was thought necessary.

The Palladian facade of the Assembly Rooms opened in Northgate Street in 1821. They later became the home of the Ipswich High School for Girls, which is now at Woolverstone Hall.

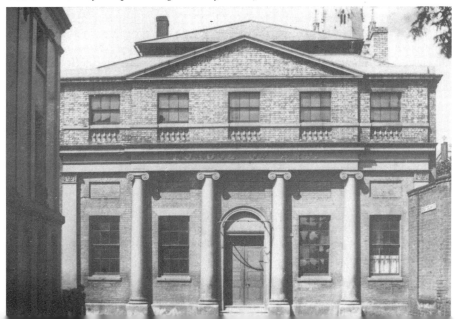

Between £3,000 and £4,000 was raised at a meeting presided over by Sir William Middleton, of Shrubland Hall, in 1818 to promote the building of New Assembly Rooms in Northgate Street, to rival the 'elegant and universally admired' Assembly Rooms at fashionable Bury St Edmunds. More funds were expected from prominent members of local society to hasten the building work, but progress was seriously delayed by a case in the Court of Chancery that sought to prevent the sale of two houses in the street to the subscribers. The case failed, but there were other difficulties ahead and the story of the New Assembly Rooms was a less-than-happy one, though the scheme certainly left its mark on the street. Not only did the white brick facade of the New Assembly Rooms with its four imposing pillars grace Northgate for many a year but the side wall of the Great White Horse Hotel was rebuilt in Suffolk whites to match.

Opened with a ball and supper in January 1821 attended by 'nearly 200 of the Nobility and principal Gentry of the county', the New Assembly Rooms had a ballroom 54ft long and 27ft wide (16 × 8m), with a room under it designed as a library and a series of other rooms such as supper room, card room and reading rooms. Sadly, though, the local nobility and gentry proved to be insufficiently generous, and there was not enough to pay for the work done. In 1827 James and Robert Ransome complained that they had never been paid for ironwork ordered eight years earlier, remarking that the building had been 'raised at the expense of the different tradesmen employed … none of whose bills, we are informed, up to the present are paid!' Two years earlier the New Assembly Rooms had been put up for sale, the advertisement pointing out that little alteration would be needed to turn them into a fine family home.

In later years the premises became the Ipswich High School for Girls, which moved elsewhere in 1907 and is now at Woolverstone Hall. Today the premises house a nightclub.
☛ *See also Coffee House, The Old*

ASWAN DAM
Sluice gates were made by Ransomes & Rapier in 1902 for the first Aswan Dam on the River Nile. This great dam across the Nile in southern Egypt was the first to be built to harness the waters of that river for the benefit of agriculture; sluices made in Ipswich by Ransomes & Rapier also went into many of the other barrages built on the Nile.
☛ *See also Ransomes & Rapier*

ATFIELD, DOUG
Antiques dealer Doug Atfield ran the shop of Atfield & Daughter in St Stephen's Lane and became locally famous when he infuriated the local

authority by erecting a bollard to prevent lorries striking the front of his building. During a long-running campaign he refused to remove the bollard, though prosecuted for obstructing the highway; in the end he was forced to remove his bollard, and it was replaced by another put in place by the borough council. In recent years he and his family have been restoring the St Stephen's Lane building, once the Sun Inn.

AYTON, FRANK

Having been resident engineer for the construction of the electric tramway in 1903, Frank Ayton was appointed engineer and manager of the Corporation Tramways. An enthusiastic proponent of electric traction, he took a keen interest when Ransomes, Sims & Jefferies began building battery-electric vehicles in 1914; two of their early battery-electric lorries are in the Ipswich Transport Museum. While tramways manager he opened a municipal charging station for the traction batteries of electric vehicles, making Ipswich the first town in the country to have such a facility. Having seen the tramways through the 1914–18 war, he resigned in 1921 to take up a new post with Ransomes, who in later years built trolleybuses. On the centenary of municipal transport in Ipswich in 2003, Ipswich Buses no. 59 was named *Frank Ayton*.
☛ **See also Ransomes, Sims & Jefferies; Trams, electric; Trolleybuses**

BACON, NATHANIELL

A grandson of Sir Nicholas Bacon, Lord Chancellor in the reign of King James I, Nathaniell Bacon accepted the invitation to become Recorder of Ipswich in 1642. At that time the corporation was struggling to maintain the Puritan cause against the Royalist faction. John Lany, a Royalist who had taken his deceased father's place as Recorder, had been discharged from that position, and two leading Puritan members of the corporation, Peter Fisher and Samuel Duncon, were sent to invite Bacon to take over the recordership. Bacon replied 'that if the town will please to make choise of him, he will comme and live in the towne'. The result was that he took up residence in St Margaret's parish and was elected Recorder at a Great Court on 30 December 1642. He was in due course also sworn in as a burgess.

When Suffolk joined with five neighbouring counties to form the Eastern Association in the winter of 1642–3, Bacon became chairman of the Cambridge Committee, which ran that association with an efficiency and self-assurance that ensured success. Ipswich played a leading part in the affairs of the Eastern Association, which soon consisted of eight counties. Bacon's handling of its affairs was responsible for maintaining order in East Anglia during the Second Civil War and preventing the spread of hostilities to this part of England. When Nathaniell had to be absent from Cambridge, his positions as Suffolk representative and chairman were taken by his brother Francis, also a lawyer. On William Cage's death in 1646, Francis Bacon was elected to represent Ipswich in Parliament.

Nine years after becoming Recorder, Nathaniell Bacon was elected Town Clerk, and in 1653 he was elected a claviger. In 1654 he was elected to represent the borough in Parliament along with his brother Francis, and they were re-elected in 1656, 1658 and 1660. Bacon became aware of the need for an up-to-date digest of the rules under which the town was governed, and he set about copying out many of the more important decisions of the Great Court and the Assembly from the court rolls. He finished his work on the records in 1649, the year in which the trial and execution of King Charles I took place. It was a procedure with which he had no sympathy whatever, and he ended his transcript with the words 'The last day of January puts a sad period unto my pen. And thus by the Goodness of Almighty God, I have summed up the affaires of the Government of This Town of Ipswich under Bayliffs; whoe are happy in this, that God hathe established their seate more sure than the throne of Kings'.

His transcript of the records was published in 1884 as *The Annalls of Ipswiche, The Lawes Customes and Government of the same collected out of the records books and writings of that towne*. On his death in 1660 the corporation granted £25 to his widow 'for the great paynes that her husband … did take in the transcribinge of several ancient Records belonging to this Towne'.

BAILIFFS

The chief officials of the corporation from the granting of the charter to the reforms of the 1830s were two bailiffs, elected each year from among 'the more lawful men' of the town. The first bailiffs, chosen at an open-air meeting in the churchyard of St Mary-le-Tower on 29 June 1200, were John fitzNorman and Robert Belines, apparently two of the group of leading citizens who had negotiated with the king's officers the granting of the charter. Early checks on the bailiffs seem to have been ineffective, since at the beginning of the thirteenth century two men almost monopolised the post over a twelve-year period. Thomas Stacey and Thomas le Rente were bailiffs in 1307–11 and 1318–20; one or the other was a bailiff in 1312, 1313, 1314 and 1316; and the rest of the time one of their associates was usually bailiff. Further checks were put in place when this local mafia was ousted in 1320, but in spite of that their successors seemed adept at mishandling local politics to their own advantage. The same propensity to use their position to benefit themselves and their own political interests was displayed by eighteenth-century bailiffs such as Cooper Gravener, who between 1702 and 1720 served twelve terms as bailiff, during which the Tories gained political advantage by making large numbers of honorary freemen and a good income from those who purchased the freedom.

☛ *See also Charter*

BARNARD, JOHN

The most prestigious and best-known of the eighteenth-century Ipswich shipbuilders, John Barnard set up his business in 1734 in one of the St Clement's yards, where his father, also John Barnard, had earlier been a shipbuilder. Within five years he was building vessels for the Royal Navy. Young John's first warship was the *Biddeford*, launched on 15 June 1740 and towed downriver to be rigged at the former Navy Yard at Harwich. A few weeks before that launching he obtained an order for a 50-gun fourth-rate, the *Hampshire*, which he built downriver at John's Ness. A third warship, the bomb vessel *Granado*, was launched in 1742. John seems to have followed his father as a member of the Dissenting congregation meeting in the Green Yard in St Peter's parish and later in the chapel in Tacket Street that succeeded the earlier meeting house about 1719. It is said that he, or possibly his mother Mary who carried on the business after her husband's death, provided old ship's masts to support the roof of the new chapel.

There is a story that when John's son William in partnership with William Dudman gained a contract for an East Indiaman, the *Speaker*, in 1762 John found himself in conflict with the Reverend William Gordon, pastor of the Tacket Street chapel. Gordon was convinced that the schedule demanded by the contract would necessitate Sunday working and began a campaign, even visiting the shipyard to persuade the workmen to refuse to work on the Sabbath if they were asked. When in December the men were asked to work on a Sunday, most of them did so, but at New Year Gordon launched a savage attack on Barnard from his pulpit for defiling the Lord's Day. It does not seem to have gone down well with the congregation. Sunday working or no, shipbuilding has always been a precarious occupation: in 1781 John Barnard, after many years of successful operation, came up against the old bugbear of insufficient cash flow and was declared bankrupt at the age of seventy-six. He went to live at Deptford with his son William, who was appointed one of his assignees, and died there in 1784.

See John E. Barnard, *Building Britain's Wooden Walls* (Anthony Nelson, 1997)

☞ *See also Gordon, Dr William; Shipyards*

BARRACKS

A local builder, Richard Gooding, built barracks for cavalry in 1795 on land to the north of the junction of St Matthew's Street, London Road and Norwich Road, later to be known as Barrack Corner. The entrance to the barracks was up a lane from St Matthew's Street; the brick buildings stood on three sides of a large parade ground, the officers' mess on one side flanked by barrack rooms for the soldiers on each side. Ipswich was well used to troops being billeted in the town, but up to that time there had not been a

Artillerymen with a muzzle-loading field gun at Ipswich Barracks about the time of the Crimean War.

permanent barracks. The first regiment to take up residence at the barracks was the 2nd or Queen's Regiment of Dragoon Guards, known as the Queen's Bays since 1762 when they were first mounted on bay horses. Other mounted regiments moved into the Horse Barracks in later years, Ipswich becoming quite a popular posting. In the second half of the nineteenth century the cavalry gave way to artillery, units of the Royal Field Artillery and Royal Horse Artillery being stationed there well into the twentieth century. The barracks were demolished in 1928, and the site is now occupied by the council houses of Geneva Road and Cecil Road.

☛ *See also St. Helen's Barracks; Stoke Barracks*

BAYLEY, JABEZ

One of the town's best-known shipbuilders, Jabez Bayley launched his most famous vessel, the East Indiaman *Orwell*, from the Halifax yard in 1817 in the presence, it was reported at the time, of 20,000 people. Contrary to popular belief, the *Orwell* was not the largest vessel built at Ipswich; this distinction was enjoyed by two further East Indiamen, the *David Scott* and the *William Fairlie*, ordered by Captain Henry Templar of Limehouse. By the time they were ready for launching, the captain had sold his contract with the Honourable East India Company to Scott, Fairlie & Hare of London, two of whose principals gave their names to the ships. Earlier Jabez had attracted orders from the Navy Board, building thirty-one warships in Ipswich between 1804 and 1814. He gained an excellent reputation for the attention he paid to ventilation and the prevention of rot. When the *Orwell* was broken up in London in 1840 the Suffolk oak of which she was built, though considered to be very green at the time it was put into her, was found to be in surprisingly good condition.

Although a good businessman and an excellent shipwright, Jabez sometimes showed a certain lack of good judgement; his nephew George described him as 'one of those good natured impulsive men on whom one cannot rely with confidence'. He came to dominate local shipbuilding and as well as running his yards at St Peter's and Halifax he leased others, but he over-reached himself and found himself in financial trouble. He had lost money on building the *Orwell*, partly because of having to dredge a deep channel from the yard out to deep water for the launching. The building of the two even bigger Indiamen and other vessels, although profitable, failed to restore his fortune. He was declared bankrupt in 1825, but seems to have been discharged from bankruptcy a couple of years later, since he built the steamer *Commerce* in 1828. He also obtained a contract to build a steam dredger for the Norwich and Lowestoft Navigation Company at Lowestoft. Jabez died in 1834.

See Hugh Moffat, *Ships and Shipyards of Ipswich 1700–1970* (Malthouse Press, 2002)

☞ *See also Shipyards*

BECK, CAVE

Master of Ipswich Grammar School from 1650 to 1657 and then incumbent of St Margaret's Church for some twenty years, Cave Beck was one of the attendant gentlemen who went to Holland with Leicester Devereux, 5th Viscount Hereford (of Christchurch Mansion) and five other peers to bring back Charles II in 1660. His unusual Christian name was derived from his mother's maiden name. He was with Charles I at Oxford, probably engaged in undercover cipher work, but in spite of his Royalist leanings he obtained the mastership of the Grammar School in 1650, apparently enjoying the friendship of some of the Puritan leaders of that period. As master, he took his responsibility for the Town Library very seriously; it was he who hit on the system of marking the fore-edge of each book with a diagonal line and a symbol to enable them to be regularly checked and kept in place without the help of an expert librarian.

After resigning from the mastership in 1657 Beck published his attempt at a universal language, based on the Arabic numbers 1 to 9. The engraved frontispiece of his book shows Beck handing a scroll bearing the numbers 2356, representing the verb 'to hunt', to an Indian in a turban, an African and a native American, the latter holding an arrow in his left hand and raising his right hand to indicate that he understands the message on the scroll.

Following the Glorious Revolution of 1688, Beck was involved with Devereux Edgar, an Ipswich magistrate, in the installation of fifty painted panels between the rafters of the double hammerbeam roof of St Margaret's Church. These panels, dating from 1694–5, celebrate the accession of

William III and Mary and the settlement of the religious troubles and the struggle between Crown and Parliament. Beck died in 1706.

☛ *See also Grammar School*

BELL, THE OLD

Said to be the oldest licensed premises in the town, the Old Bell Inn 'Over Stoke' stands at the junction of Stoke Street and Vernon Street, with Bell Lane running up on its west side, now truncated by the building of council flats in Bell Close. The existing timber-framed building is much smaller than the original, part of the east end having been demolished to make way for Vernon Street.

☛ *See also Vernon Street*

BELLFOUNDERS

The earliest record of church bells being cast in Ipswich dates from the second half of the seventeenth century, when John Darbie from Kelsale set up a bell foundry in St Clement's parish. Unlike his brother Michael, who became an itinerant bellfounder and ruined more than one medieval peal by recasting the bells, John Darbie has a good reputation among campanologists, casting 158 bells for Suffolk churches between 1658 and 1691. Among them was the ring of six in St Clement's, Ipswich, which were rehung by a later Ipswich bellfounder, Alfred Bowell, in the twentieth century. Alfred Bowell's father Henry moved to Ipswich in 1852 and served a seven-year apprenticeship as a shipwright, but with the decline in wooden shipbuilding on the Orwell he turned to bell-hanging. Alfred followed and for some years the business was known as H. Bowell & Son, with premises in Wykes Bishop Street; when his father died in 1913 the firm became simply Alfred Bowell. Alfred cast bells for churches right across the country, and rehung many existing bells; he also repaired or reconstructed many church clocks. The last bell, for a church in Cambridgeshire, was made during the Second World War.

BELSTEAD BROOK

Rising near the Copdock interchange, the Belstead Brook flows about two and a half miles eastwards to join the Orwell at Ostrich Creek. For part of its course it forms the boundary between Stoke and Wherstead, first set down in Anglo-Saxon in 970. The boundary document suggests that there was then a watermill near where the Stoke boundary strikes off to the north, and later there was certainly another mill at Bourne Bridge, close to where it flows into the Orwell. Today the land bordering the stream has become the Belstead Brook Park and is managed by the Greenways Project as an informal country park where people can enjoy a taste of the countryside close to their homes.

☛ *See also Greenways Project*

BETHESDA

The imposing frontage of the Bethesda Baptist Church, with its pediment supported by four tall columns, dates from 1913 but the church was

established in 1829 when twenty-nine members left the Stoke Green Baptist Church to form another congregation. They first met in a small chapel in St Clement's and then took over a disused Independent chapel in what was then known as Dairy Lane, now Fonnereau Road. Their first pastor, James Nunn, seems to have had business in London during the week and travelled to Ipswich each weekend to take services, no easy task in pre-railway days. The new chapel was funded by Mr Arthur Page, a Bristol lawyer, as a memorial to his mother, who died in 1911 at the age of eighty-two; she had been baptised in the Orwell sixty-seven years before by James Nunn. The congregation held their final service in the old chapel in the last week of 1911, and the much larger new one was opened on 2 July 1913. Arthur Page deliberately stayed away from the

The imposing façade of the Bethesda Baptist Church can be seen in this photograph taken looking up Northgate Street past the site of the old North Gate.

opening ceremony and the first services as he felt it was inappropriate that any thanks should be given to him. In 2000 the church branched out by acquiring premises on St Margaret's Plain which had been the Running Buck; after refurbishment they opened as The Key, a centre for outreach activities.

See Frederick G. Smith, *The Bethesda Story* (1963)
☞ *See also Dairy Lane; Fonnereau Road*

BLACKFRIARS

The excavated remains of the church of the Dominican friars or Blackfriars are to be seen between Foundation Street and Lower Orwell Street. Although many of the friary buildings were put to other uses, the church was demolished quite soon after the Dissolution of the religious houses by Henry VIII. Unlike monks, who spent much of their time managing their estates as

The great preaching church of the Blackfriars had been demolished and cleared away long before Joshua Kirby produced his picture of the surviving parts of the Blackfriars in 1748. The most prominent building in this view is the refectory.

well as in prayer, the friars devoted themselves to a life of poverty, self-sacrifice and active well-doing, and to preaching the gospel as taught by the Vatican. The Blackfriars became established in Ipswich in 1263, when the house of Hugh de Langeston was acquired for them by Henry III. Parts of that stone house survived the Dissolution, but it was demolished with the rest of the Blackfriars in the mid-nineteenth century. The great preaching church, dedicated to St Mary, had a length of 177 feet (54m), and the nave alone was 98ft long and 50ft wide (30 × 15m). It had disappeared long before Joshua Kirby drew a plan and prospect of the Blackfriars buildings in 1748, causing historians endless confusion as some assumed that the refectory, prominent in Kirby's prospect, was the former church.

BLACK HORSE LANE
Running from Westgate Street just inside the West Gate to Elm Street, this lane took its name from the Black Horse public house on its east side. This hostelry, erected in the sixteenth century, is among the town's older surviving buildings. It closed in the 1970s but then reopened, and today enjoys a thriving trade from the nearby Civic Centre and business premises. In the seventeenth and eighteenth centuries the lane was called Burstall Lane; after the transfer of the borough prison from the west gate to two houses on the east side of the lane (pulled down in 1822), it was also called Gaol Lane or Old Gaol Lane. The earlier and later names both appear on Pennington's map of 1776.

BLAKE, JOHN LE
There is some uncertainty whether this gentleman is properly known as John the Black, perhaps a man with jet-black hair, or as Black John, the man who

caused the corporation a good deal of trouble. He was the Town Clerk who fled from justice in September 1272. We do not know his crimes, but there is a strong suspicion of embezzlement. It was probably to deprive the authorities of the evidence against him that he took out of the hutch or town chest certain town records. Among these was le Domesday, Ipswich's own book of the laws and free customs of the town; alas, neither John nor the archive was ever seen again, so far as we know.

It seems to have taken nearly twenty years before the town saw need to replace the missing documents. It was ordained that the customs and constitution of the town authorities be 'again brought into writing', and twenty-four of the most responsible citizens were given the task of setting the facts down, presumably from memory. That is how Ipswich is today in the happy position of having various copies of its earliest records. Professor Geoffrey Martin, who knows more about the Ipswich records than anyone else, points out that it is likely that the delinquency of the common clerk was responsible not so much for the loss of the original records as for the survival of the town's later medieval archives.

See G.H. Martin, *The Early Court Rolls of the Borough of Ipswich* (University College of Leicester, 1954)

☞ *See also Charter*

BLUE COAT SCHOOL

A girls' charity school associated with the Grey Coat School for boys, the Blue Coat School was opened in 1710. While education was considered

essential in setting boys on the path of life and religion, the teaching of girls was regarded as of secondary importance. In 1737 a resolution was passed by those in charge of the Blue Coat School that 'Whereas the girls have for some years past been taught to write at considerable expense, without the written order of the Governors, it is now ordered that no girls henceforth be taught to write at the expense of the Society'.

This plaque is a reminder of the old Blue Coat and Grey Coat schools, in Curriers Lane.

BOAT LANE

An early name, found on both Ogilby's and Pennington's maps, for the roadway leading to Friars Bridge, even earlier known as Botflud. By the nineteenth century it had become known as Friars Bridge Road.

BOER WAR MEMORIAL

The South African War Memorial, erected on Cornhill at the front of the Town Hall, commemorated the men of the Suffolk Regiment who had fallen in the fighting in South Africa and East Suffolk men who had died serving there with other regiments. It was unveiled on 29 September 1906 by General Sir John French in the presence of large crowds, many of whom watched from windows above the Cornhill shops and Head Post Office. Designed by sculptor Alfred Toft, the memorial depicts a soldier, his rifle reversed in mourning, standing by the grave of a comrade. It was later moved to Christchurch Park, where it stands near the Cenotaph erected after the First World War.

☛ *See also Christchurch Mansion; Cornhill*

BOSS HALL

Now the site of a retail park off Sproughton Road, Boss Hall is on the north bank of the Gipping and on the western outskirts of the town. Roman pottery has been found, and there was probably a river crossing here in Roman times and certainly later. The name Pottaford given in the Anglo-Saxon bounds of Stoke in 970 is likely to be derived from Roman pottery exposed as the riverbank was eroded on the outside of the bend. Later references are to Bordshaw Hall, presumably the house that occupied a fourteenth-century moated site; Edward de Bordshawe was lord of Boos Hall (so spelt) in the reign of Henry III. The hall was demolished in the 1970s. In 1990 an early Anglo-Saxon cemetery was discovered during building work. An excavation by the Suffolk Archaeological Unit revealed nineteen graves; another three graves and a cremation urn were found in pipe and cable trenches near the main site. All but one of the graves were from the sixth and early seventh centuries; the exception, that of a wealthy woman whose garnet-set brooch and other objects were buried with her in a bag, dated from about 700. The brooch, four gold disc-shaped pendants, a silver cosmetic set, two coins and various other smaller pendants and beads were lifted from the grave by the archaeologists in a small block of soil and taken to the British Museum, where Fleur Shearman skilfully disentangled them. As a result of an appeal they were later purchased for the Ipswich Museum.

BOTWOOD'S

The firm established in 1870 by William Botwood grew into a large carriage-building concern that exported carriages and even rickshaws to the far corners of the Empire. The premises on the Woodbridge Road, between Kirby Street and Milton Street, remained the manufactory for many years, but in 1882 showrooms were opened in St Matthew's Street. When William Botwood died in 1896, the business was carried on by two of his sons,

Samuel Ernest and William Thomas Botwood, who a few years later were joined by a famous pioneer motorist, Reginald Egerton. Together they formed a new firm of Botwood & Egerton, motor-car manufacturers and engineers, and motor cab proprietors, which operated alongside that of W.T. & S.E. Botwood, carriage-builders. In 1910 Egerton left the partnership to set up his own business in Northgate, next to the Great White Horse Hotel, and the Botwood business then became Botwoods Ltd. In the 1920s the Botwood shares were acquired by Mann, Egerton & Co, of Norwich, who had by then expanded to premises at the town end of Woodbridge Road. In 1924 Botwoods, who continued to trade under their own name until about 1970, moved their showrooms from Carr Street to Majors Corner.

See John F. Bridges, *Early Country Motoring* (1995)
☛ *See also Egerton, Reginald*

BOY BISHOP
Before the Reformation it was traditional in Ipswich as in many other places for a boy bishop to be appointed on St Nicholas's Day, 6 December. In Ipswich he was probably a pupil of the Grammar School, since one of the complaints against Richard Argentine, master of the school from 1538 to 1558, was that he led 'the boy St Nicholas with his miniver hood about the streets, for apples and bellie-cheer'. The boy bishop remained in office until Holy Innocents' Day, 28 December, the commemoration of the slaughter of the children by King Herod and regarded for centuries as the unluckiest day of the year. This was no mere piece of fun but a serious rite: during his brief reign the boy bishop was treated with all due respect and participated in services, even having to preach a sermon on Holy Innocents' Day. In England the practice of appointing a boy bishop was suppressed by royal proclamation in 1541, though the Catholic Queen Mary restored it three years later; it was again forbidden by Queen Elizabeth I.
☛ *See also Argentine, Richard*

BRICKMAKING
The London clay (its geological name) found in the Ipswich area makes excellent bricks. In 1589, Henry Wiseman of Ipswich was described as a brickstriker; the action of cutting off the waste clay or pug from the top of the brick in the mould is known as 'striking off'. Among his effects were both burnt and unburnt bricks and 'pavements' or paving bricks as well as loads of logs, brushwood and whins, presumably for firing the kiln. Perhaps Wiseman was working the brickyard in the east of Ipswich that appears on Ogilby's seventeenth-century map as 'Claypitt for Brick & tyle'. It might have been the same yard from which William Robinson advertised in 1771 'fine Rubbing Bricks and black Cornice, red Pantiles and glazed ditto, and all sorts of Bricks

Taken about 1905, this photograph shows one of the Ipswich brickworks that supplied bricks and tiles for the expansion of the town. This one, with its rows of drying sheds, stood on Hog Highland where Cliff Quay is now.

and Tyles'. Rubbing bricks or 'rubbers' were soft, fine-textured bricks that could be abraded to shape by the bricklayer; they can be seen over the windows of Georgian houses and in other positions where special shapes were required.

In the nineteenth century many more brickyards sprang up, one of them – between Back Hamlet and Fore Hamlet – being known as the Trinity Brickworks; the claypit of this works was later the site of Ransomes' aircraft works, the White City. Others were the Valley Brickworks in Foxhall Road, another between Woodbridge Road and Spring Road, one in Stoke, the Broom Hill brickworks east of the Norwich Road, and one on Hog Highland. The last to work was Bolton's brickworks in The Dales, which turned out its final batch of bricks in 1958; this big works, together with the Grove brickworks to the east, which closed much earlier, was served by a railway branch from the East Suffolk Line near Westerfield station. The parapet of the bridge that carried Henley Road over the line is still to be seen near Henley Grove.

BROKES HALL

The moated house known as Brokes or Brooks Hall disappeared early in the twentieth century and the site now lies beneath Valley Road, part of the original Ipswich bypass. Its origin lay in the holding known as Brokes, given by Edward the Confessor to Aluric de Clare and later held by Robert de Badele of the Earl of Clare by one knight's fee. It seems that Robert gave

The pond on the east side of Norwich Road, seen here in a photograph said to have been taken in 1869, was part of the old moat of Brokes Hall. It eventually disappeared when houses were built on that side of the road.

Brokes to St Peter's Church in Ipswich; the church also held 91 acres in Thurleston, which could have adjoined part of Brokes. There are references to properties in Brookes or Brokes in the Cartulary of the Priory of SS Peter and Paul. Other documents refer to Geoffrey de Badele, who in the reign of Henry III was lord of the manor of Badley, near Needham Market, under the Honour of Clare.

☛ *See also St Peter's Church*

BROOK STREET

Running from the White Horse Corner to a junction with Foundation Street, Brook Street (now divided into Upper and Lower portions at Dog's Head Street/Tacket Street) takes its name from the stream that formerly flowed down from the springs and ponds in Christchurch Park to reach the river below Stoke Bridge.

The premises of Alexander the Great Clothier on the corner of Upper Brook Street and Tacket Street, seen in the 1930s.

Although the stream disappeared long ago, presumably culverted, flooding occurred from time to time when heavy rainfall swelled the ponds in the park. One bitterly cold night in January 1848 W.C. Fonnereau of Christchurch saved the situation, when fire broke out at the printing office of the *Ipswich Express* in the Buttermarket, by opening the sluices of his ponds and sending a cascade of water down into Brook Street to supply the fire engines.

BRUFF, PETER

Peter Schuyler Bruff is sometimes called 'the Brunel of the Eastern Counties', for he was involved in railway building and a wide range of other engineering projects in the region. Having trained as an engineer under Joseph Locke, probably when Locke was working under George Stephenson on the Liverpool and Manchester Railway, Bruff came to East Anglia as a surveyor under John Braithwaite on the Eastern Counties Railway. Even then Bruff was working on a scheme for extending the line to Ipswich, which caught the attention of John Cobbold and his son John Chevallier Cobbold. The result was that Bruff became engineer of the Eastern Union Railway, which was almost entirely promoted and initially financed in Ipswich. He built the line between Colchester and Ipswich, then the line to Bury, and extended it from Stowmarket to Norwich. Faced with a quaking bog near Stowmarket that swallowed enormous quantities of earth dug from a cutting just north of the town, as well as sections of line, Bruff overcame the problem by floating the embankment on a raft of faggots and brushwood, as did Stephenson at Chat Moss. The Eastern Union had to fight the bitter hostility of the Eastern Counties, which made every effort to prevent convenient connections at Colchester. As manager of the Eastern Union, Bruff had to contend with constant harassment from the rival company; at one stage he and Cobbold resorted to running a steam-packet service between Ipswich and London.

When the Eastern Counties took over the running of the Eastern Union, Bruff entered the service of the former rival, at first as engineer and superintendent of the Eastern Union section, then of the whole system from November 1854. His health broke down in 1856, and he resigned the following year. It was by no means the end of Bruff's career, however. He was involved in the development of the Essex seaside resorts of Walton-on-the-Naze, Frinton and Clacton-on-Sea and with the building of several more railway lines. In 1863 he was appointed engineer to the Harwich Harbour Conservancy Board, a post he held for thirty-two years. In 1857 he had been asked to design a drainage system for Ipswich, which he did; but the expense was considered too great and nothing was done until 1881–2, when a main low-level sewer was constructed through the heart of the town to outfall tanks on the bank of the Orwell at a cost of £60,000. Bruff died at his Ipswich home, Handford Lodge, Handford Road, in 1900. He was then the father of the Institution of Civil Engineers, to which he had been elected nearly sixty years earlier.

See Hugh Moffat, *East Anglia's First Railways* (Terence Dalton, 1987)
☛ *See also Railway, Eastern Union*

BUILDING PRESERVATION TRUST, IPSWICH

Few historic towns in Britain have suffered more loss of ancient buildings than Ipswich. The process had certainly started by 1818 when the front of the Great White Horse Hotel and other timber-framed buildings in Tavern Street were sacrificed to add a few feet to the width of the street, and it has continued even into the twenty-first century. The Ipswich Building Preservation Trust Ltd was formed in 1978 to preserve buildings of historical, architectural or constructional interest that might be at risk of falling down through dilapidation or of being demolished for redevelopment.

Various properties have been restored by the trust, including Pykenham's Gatehouse in Northgate, an attractive little seventeenth-century house in Bolton Lane and the former Half Moon and Star in St Matthew's Street. The

The former Half Moon and Star in St Matthew's Street is one of the buildings saved by the trust.

trust was originally financed by an interest-free loan from the borough council which enabled it to acquire its first property, and it has gradually built up its assets by selling restored buildings to finance the purchase and restoration of further properties.

Projects undertaken by the trust do not compete with what private individuals or commercial undertakings might be able to achieve. The intention is to carry out restorations that are not commercially attractive and thus to save buildings that might otherwise be lost.

BULL-BAITING

In medieval times the baiting of bulls by dogs was not just a cruel sport enjoyed by heartless spectators, for it was thought that baiting in some way improved the meat. Butchers who failed to have their bulls baited for at least an hour before slaughtering found themselves penalised by the town authorities, who imposed fines for what was considered a serious breach of the town regulations. Bulls were tethered to a ring in the middle of the Cornhill to be baited before being slaughtered in the Shambles nearby.

☛ *See also Cornhill; Shambles, The*

BULL GATE

As part of a general refurbishment of the town defences in 1603, a new gate was added where an existing path from Westgate Street to Clay Street crossed the rampart. The new gate apparently took its name from Anthony Bull, a portman, who had 'a little house' there. The name is not on Ogilby's map but it is found on Pennington's, even if it seems to apply to the lane rather than to a barrier at the end of it. Later this lane was known as Barley Mow Lane after the tavern at its corner with Clay Lane, but in the nineteenth century it

took a new name, High Street, and was extended on the north side of Clay Lane to link up with the newly developed Fonnereau Road.
☛ *See also Clay Lane; East Gate; Ogilby, John; Pennington, Joseph; Walls, town; West Gate*

BULL MOTORS

Napier Prentice, a member of the family that was for many years concerned with making agricultural fertilisers and explosives at Stowmarket, began the manufacture of quiet-running DC electric motors in 1898. He had earlier constructed generators both for the supply of current to the family fertiliser works and for public supply at Stowmarket, Diss and Felixstowe, and he set up the East Anglian Electric Supply Company, which brought mains electricity to several parts of Suffolk in the 1920s and 1930s. He formed the East Anglian Engineering Company at Stowmarket to produce Bull Motors, and this company moved to E. R. & F. Turner's St Peter's Works in Ipswich in 1924. The company made electric motors for trolleybuses built by Ransomes, Sims & Jefferies at Orwell Works and for mobile cranes made by Ransomes & Rapier at Waterside Works, as well as motors for blowing church organs and operating passenger and goods lifts in shops and industrial buildings. Bull Motors became part of E. R. & F. Turner in the 1930s, but later became a separate company again, operating from a works in Foxhall Road. It closed at the end of the twentieth century.
☛ *See also Orwell Works; Ransomes & Rapier; Ransomes, Sims & Jefferies; Turner, E.R. & F.*

BULL, RANSOMES'

The plough works of Ransomes, Sims & Jefferies and the Waterside Works of Ransomes & Rapier had a steam whistle, known popularly as 'the Bull'. Another was used by William Pretty & Sons to call workers to the corset factory in Tower Ramparts. The Stoke Bull at Waterside Works was the most resonant of the trio and was operated in the early 1920s by the furnaceman, Thomas Prentice, who 'pulled' it at 7.45, 7.55 and 8am and again at 1.50, 1.55 and 2pm for restarting work after the dinner break. In 1927 this Bull was replaced by a Kockums Air Typhoon, a Swedish compressed-air siren like that on the liner *Gripsholm*. This was sounded by William Silburn and George Thirkettle. It was last used in the early hours of 4 September 1939, when it was sounded as an air-raid warning. It was not reinstated after the war, but the plough works Bull did resume its bellows, being sounded each day by the lodge keeper, until it was silenced in the 1950s because of complaints from people living near by. Another steam whistle, at the fertiliser works at Bramford, could, if the wind was right, be clearly heard in the town when it 'went off' at 7am.
☛ *See also Pretty, William, & Sons; Ransomes & Rapier; Ransomes, Sims & Jefferies*

BUNTING, HMS

This was the Second World War naval base at Cliff Quay; it began life in July 1940 as part of HMS *Badger* at Parkeston Quay. Cliff Quay served throughout the war as a base for patrol trawlers and naval launches operating in the North Sea, a very lively theatre of war. The name *Bunting* was adopted in September 1940 when HMS *Bunting*, the former steam yacht *Merlin* built in Glasgow in 1897, was sent to Ipswich as base ship. Two other ships were given the name *Bunting* during the war: the motor yacht *Freelance* and the South Coast paddle steamer *Emperor of India* which came to Ipswich as an accommodation ship in 1943. Another naval base in the Ipswich area was HMS *Woolverstone*, a combined operations base occupying Woolverstone Hall and the surrounding park.

☞ *See also Cliff Quay*

BURSTALL LANE

☞ *See Black Horse Lane*

BUTTERMARKET

This highway running from Queen Street to Upper Brook Street was not always so called. The name first appeared in 1621, and in 1635 it was 'the fish market now used as the butter market', but even then it applied only to a small section of the street. Throughout the eighteenth century the east end of the street was called 'the street from the Butter Market to Brook Street'. It

The junction of Queen Street and the Buttermarket, a photograph taken in the 1970s. The Giles family statue now stands just about where someone is crossing the road.

was probably not until the butter market ceased to be held there that the name was applied to the entire street. In the 1860s tradesmen in the Buttermarket decided to widen the east end of the street, and after they 'had succeeded in inducing the Local Board of Health to vote £2,000 for the piece of land to be thrown into the street' they bought a number of properties on the north side and replaced them with a row of 'good-looking white and red brick houses'. Some confusion was caused in the 1990s when a new shopping centre west of St Stephen's Lane and north of the Old Cattle Market was named Buttermarket Centre; buses using the Old Cattle Market bus station even bore destination boards saying 'Buttermarket'. When people complained that using the name Buttermarket for the Old Cattle Market was confusing, a local politician declared that we could not go on using old-fashioned names: we must accept new names, like Buttermarket.

See Muriel Clegg, *Streets and Street names in Ipswich* (Salient Press, 1984)

CABMEN'S SHELTER
Erected on the Cornhill and opened on 23 January 1893, the timber-framed shelter was intended as a refuge from bad weather for the men from the cab rank. It was, however, alleged that they congregated in the shelter and ignored would-be passengers. The building was therefore removed to Christchurch Park on 16 May 1895, on a trolley towed through the streets by the corporation steam-roller. It survived near the Bolton Lane entrance to the park for a century, but was seriously damaged in an arson attack.
☞ *See also Christchurch Mansion; Cornhill*

CALIFORNIA
This name was given to part of the old Cauldwell Hall estate purchased on behalf of the Ipswich & Suffolk Freehold Land Society in 1849, the year of the California Gold Rush. Plots were allocated to its members by the drawing of lots, and these plots were at first used not for building houses but as smallholdings. There is a story that James Calver, a one-time Chartist who had lost his investment in an earlier National Freehold Land Society, was working on his allotment when 'a great man of the town' rode up on his horse and asked 'What are you digging there for?' Calver did not like the way the question was asked, and replied somewhat acidly 'Digging for gold, the way they do in California.' That might, or might not, be the origin of the name California later given to that area of the expanding town. The area is now better known as St John's, after the parish church erected in Cauldwell Hall Road to serve the growing community.
☞ *See also Freehold Land Society, Ipswich & Suffolk*

CARR STREET

Part of what might have been a road from the fort at Walton to the Roman settlement of Combretovium at Baylham, Carr Street seems to have been blocked at its eastern end when the first town bank was raised by the Danes during their occupation in the early tenth century; there was no gate at that point. The origin of the name is somewhat obscure, though it seems likely to have come from a personal name; a William Caa appears in a jury list of the reign of Edward I (1272–1307). In the late sixteenth century it was 'Carre Street alias Cady Street' at a time when the Cady family was prominent in the town.

In the eighteenth century, however, this highway was generally referred to as Cross Keys Street, from an inn of that name, though both Ogilby and Pennington use the name Carr Street on their maps.

The coming of the horse tramway and a general enthusiasm for improvement led to the appearance of Carr Street being radically changed by the Carr Street Improvement Company, formed in 1887 to buy old properties and demolish them to allow widening of the street. It changed again when the Victorian buildings were replaced in 1967 by the Eastgates shopping precinct on the north side; and new shops have been built on the other side.

☞ *See also Eastgates; Ogilby, John; Pennington, Joseph; Trams, horse*

CASTLE

In the twelfth century Ipswich had a castle, but it was demolished after its capture by King Stephen in 1153 – the destruction was such that in 1735 John Kirby said it was 'so entirely demolished, that not the least Rubbish of it is to be found'. Very little is known about the castle: possibly it was a royal castle occupied by Hugh Bigod, or it may have been built by Bigod as one of the 'adulterine' castles erected by the barons without royal sanction during the eighteen years of almost continuous warfare between Henry I's daughter (and heir) Matilda and his nephew Stephen. The Anglo-Saxon Chronicle tells how the barons 'filled the whole land with these castles. They sorely burdened the unhappy people of the country with forced labour on the castles. And when the castles were made they filled them with devils and wicked men.'

John Kirby said in his book *The Suffolk Traveller* that the castle at Ipswich was torn down in 1176 on the orders of Henry II, along with that at Framlingham, but there is no known evidence to support this statement. More likely it was destroyed almost immediately after being captured by Stephen's army.

Various sites have been suggested for the castle outside the town, but none seems to fulfil the main requirements of a Norman fortification: to control the river crossing and the main entrance to the town, and to establish the owner's authority over the townsfolk. County Archaeologist Keith Wade has suggested a site in the town that does satisfy these criteria. He points out that the Saxon settlement was laid out on a grid pattern, with the streets aligned roughly north–south and east–west, a pattern largely unchanged until Victorian times. Elm Street does not fit into this pattern, however. It must originally have run west to link up with Handford Road, but has been diverted to run southward from near the Cornhill, curving west past St Mary Elms Church.

What caused this diversion of the Saxon street if not the earthworks of a motte-and-bailey castle? Further evidence for the existence of a castle here comes from a name, The Mount, used until the mid-twentieth century for the area now occupied by the police station. One wonders if this could be a folk-memory of the flattened remnants of a castle mound.

See Robert Malster, *A History of Ipswich* (Phillimore, 2000)

CASTLE HILL VILLA

The Roman villa at Castle Hill, investigated in 2004 by television's *Time Team*, was first excavated in the nineteenth century, when a patterned mosaic floor was lifted and put on display in Ipswich Museum. There are other villas in Suffolk, but this one is by far the largest and most richly decorated Roman building of its kind in the county and might well have been the home of a wealthy farmer or a provincial official. It was almost certainly the centre of a farming operation, but it was much more than just a farmhouse. Between 1946 and 1950 the site was investigated by Basil Brown, the archaeologist who discovered the Sutton Hoo ship burial, and the bath-house and other features were excavated by Judith Plouviez in 1989.

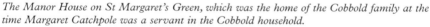

The Manor House on St Margaret's Green, which was the home of the Cobbold family at the time Margaret Catchpole was a servant in the Cobbold household.

CATCHPOLE, MARGARET
A strong-willed servant girl in the household of John Cobbold, Margaret Catchpole became perhaps the most popularly famous Suffolk person of all time when she stole her master's strawberry roan and rode off to London. The story of how she was sentenced to death at the Suffolk Assizes at Bury St Edmunds in 1797 for horse-stealing and of how she later escaped from Ipswich Gaol 'in the absence of the Keeper, who was attending his duty at Bury Assizes' by scaling the prison wall with a clothes line is well known. Recaptured, she was again sentenced to death, but that was commuted to transportation. It is said that Mrs Elizabeth Cobbold wrote pleading for her life; certainly she carried on a lively correspondence with her former servant after she had been transported to Australia. That much is true, but Margaret was not the nubile young girl of popular imagination; at the time she committed her crimes she was a mature woman of thirty-five, and when she made her escape from Ipswich Gaol the *Police Gazette* described her as plain and swarthy. The swashbuckling tale of her love affair with the smuggler Will Watch and much else came from the rich imagination of the Reverend Richard Cobbold, who when he chose her as the heroine of his first and most successful novel embroidered the facts with a great deal of fiction. Margaret died in New South Wales in 1819, having caught a fatal illness from a farmworker she was nursing.
☛ *See also Cobbold, John; Cobbold, The Reverend Richard*

CENTRAL CINEMA
One of a chain of cinemas created by Frederick Holmes Cooper, East Anglia's early cinema magnate, the Central Cinema in Princes Street opened on 8 February 1914 with a programme that included a Western featuring Bronco Bill. Unlike other Ipswich cinemas, the Central showed films throughout its life, though it did close for a time during 1937. The end came suddenly on 23 February 1950, when fire destroyed not only the Central Cinema but other adjacent properties in Princes Street.

See Stephen Peart, *The Picture House in East Anglia* (Terence Dalton, 1980)
☛ *See also Princes Street*

CHAPMAN, WILLIAM (1749–1832)
A civil engineer from Newcastle-upon-Tyne, William Chapman was called in by the businessmen and shipowners of Ipswich to advise on moves to improve the Orwell and the port of Ipswich. He had been assistant to William Jessop on the Grand Canal in Ireland and had made improvements to the River Hull in the East Riding of Yorkshire; about the time he first came to Ipswich he summed up his experience in his book *Observations of the Various Systems of Canal Navigation*. In his first report to the Committee of Subscribers for the

Improvement of the Port of Ipswich, in 1797, he proposed either a ship canal along the north side of the Orwell to bypass the shallows at Downham Bridge and the tortuous channels in the upper reaches, or dredging to straighten the channel and increase the tide in the upper reaches. His scheme was, however, considered too expensive.

Nothing was done until 1803, when it was proposed at a public meeting in the Moot Hall that Chapman's advice should be sought again. He recommended 'the formation of a Wet Dock in front of the town that may accommodate at least 100 Sail of Vessels and of a Canal Communication with it from a Lock near Downham Reach capable of admitting ships of above 370 tons measurement or near 500 tons Burthen with sufficient depth of Water for them to Navigate independently of the tides.' If that was too expensive, the river could be deepened and the channel straightened to enable vessels of 250 tons to reach the quay, but only on spring tides. Such a scheme would cost only £15,000, but he warned that 'when done your expences would not cease, because of a considerable annual charge in keeping the River to its depth, of which the advantage of ballasting the ships will form but a small part'. In other words, the material dredged from the river could be sold as ballast for ships leaving without cargo; the monopoly of supplying ballast was held by the corporation.

Faced with opposition from short-sighted people who saw every plan to improve the port as a waste of money, he scaled down his plans several times. When an Act was obtained to set up River Commissioners, he stayed to advise them on the purchase of a steam dredger, one of the first in this country. Chapman died in 1832, a few years before Ipswich embarked on building a dock remarkably similar to that which he had proposed more than thirty years earlier.

☛ *See also River Commissioners; Wet Dock*

CHARTER
Up to the end of the twelfth century, Ipswich was governed by the king's officials, but in 1200 King John granted the town a charter conferring on it the status and privileges of a free borough, enabling the townsfolk to elect their own officials. The chief of these officials were the two bailiffs; the first to be elected were John fitzNorman and Robert Belines. Ipswich was one of the first English towns to be granted the privilege of having two bailiffs elected by the inhabitants in common council, and was also among the first to be allowed a merchants' gild to organise the town's trade, with an alderman of the gild at its head.

The king did not come to Ipswich to present the charter, contrary to the general belief fostered by the official celebrations in the year 2000. He was in France at the time the charter was sealed at Roche d'Orival, near Rouen, on

Ipswich celebrates the eight-hundredth anniversary of its Charter with a civic procession including civic heads from other boroughs; the pageantry is ignored by shoppers intent on more mundane activities.

25 May 1200, and the document would have been brought to Ipswich by a herald. On 29 June 1200 the townspeople gathered in St Mary-le-Tower churchyard to elect the bailiffs and the four coroners, and then on 2 July the twelve portmen were chosen. At that second meeting the men of the town took an oath of obedience to the bailiffs, coroners and portmen and swore to uphold the honour, liberties and free customs of the town, a Bible being held aloft and the townsmen stretching their right hands towards it as they repeated the oath.

Ipswich is one of few towns to have preserved an account of what happened when the charter was received and of how local people met and decided the way in which their town should be governed in the future. Although the original town records were lost when an early town clerk decamped with the contents of the town chest in 1272, the story of the churchyard meetings and the regulations made at subsequent meetings were set down in later copies that have survived. This detailed record is something of which Ipswich should be extremely proud.

See G.H. Martin, *The Early Court Rolls of the Borough of Ipswich* (University College of Leicester, 1954)

☛ *See also Bailiffs; Freemen; Portmen*

CHEAPSIDE

Never heard now, Cheapside was an old name for the junction of Princes Street and Queen Street. When Thomas Tilling first introduced his buses into Ipswich in 1919, these ran from Cheapside, by way of the Buttermarket,

Upper Brook Street and Great Colman Street. One incautious upper-deck passenger was swept overboard by an overhanging shop sign as the bus negotiated the narrower part of the Buttermarket, and the corporation then moved the terminus to the Falcon Street and Dog's Head Street side of the Old Cattle Market.

☞ *See also Buttermarket*

CHINA, FIRST RAILWAY IN

When in 1869 the railway department of Ransomes was transferred to a new company with works on the Stoke side of the New Cut, the partners in the new business were Robert James Ransome and Richard Rapier. The latter had an ambition to build the first railway in China. His first attempt failed when it was vetoed by the Foreign Office; his suggestion that a line should be built as a wedding present to the Emperor of China was turned down on the grounds that the gesture would be misinterpreted by the Chinese as no more than the Emperor's right to exact tribute from foreign monarchs. However, in 1872 one of the leading China merchants, the firm of Jardine, Mathieson & Co., received permission from the Chinese authorities to build a quay and erect warehouses at Woosung, on the Yangtse River some twelve miles below Shanghai, and to construct a road from Shanghai to Woosung. Rapier suggested that instead of a road the firm would do better to lay a narrow-gauge railway line; the Ipswich company would engineer the line, and provide rolling-stock and the expertise to run it. Negotiations between the firms went ahead, and in due course Rapier's proposal was accepted.

A tiny locomotive, *Pioneer*, was designed and built at Waterside Works, and in 1875 five Ipswich workmen travelled out to China with it in the SS *Glenroy*. They were: the foreman, John Sadler; the chief engineer, Will Jackson; the second engineer, David Banks; the second foreman, John Sadler, jnr; and his brother George, general assistant. Theirs was no easy task, for an extreme climate and long hours of arduous work caused them severe health problems that were to cost the senior John Sadler his life. By the time he died in September 1876, half the line had been laid and a passenger service had begun, using an Ipswich-built tank engine named *Celestial Empire*. Then George Sadler became ill, and had to be sent home under the care of his brother John; that left Will Jackson and David Banks to complete the task, aided rather uncertainly by a team of Chinese labourers. Nonetheless, the line was completed and the service operated for a time, a second Ipswich-built engine, the *Flowery Land*, coming into operation in 1877.

The Ipswich men's difficulties were not over. A diplomatic incident resulted when a train decapitated a depressed Chinaman who had lain down on the line; further problems eventually resulted in closure. The original agreement had included an option for the local mandarins to purchase the

The Shanghai depot of the Woosung Tramway with one of the Ipswich-built engines on the turntable.

railway if they wished; in October 1877 the necessary cash was handed over and the mandarins acquired the line. It was immediately announced that the line would be closed on the arrival at Shanghai of the 7pm train from Woosung that very evening. It is said that the line was torn up and thrown into the river, along with the rolling-stock and equipment. Thus did the wily mandarins outwit the Foreign Devils.

On their return from China, neither Banks nor Jackson returned to Waterside Works; perhaps they feared being sent back to China or to some even more outlandish place. Banks went to the Marine Workshops at Parkeston Quay and Jackson became locomotive superintendent on the Southwold Railway. Could it be that the stories Jackson told of life in China led to the persistent legend that the Ransomes & Rapier engines were brought back to run between Halesworth and Southwold? In spite of its being found in the firm's official history this is no more than legend, though some mystery does still surround the final destination of the Woosung Railway's rolling-stock.

☛ *See also Ransomes & Rapier; Rapier, Richard*

CHIPPERFIELD, DON (1918–1992)
Well-known as a maker of local films, Don Chipperfield spent his working life with Ransomes, Sims & Jefferies, which he joined straight from school. He acquired his first camera while still at school, and one of his first cine-films of Ipswich was shot in 1933 when he was only fifteen. Unlike so many cine-photographers of the day who filmed only their family or special events, he began filming street scenes showing trolleybuses approaching the railway station along Princes Street or manoeuvring in Cornhill, then the focus of public transport in the town.

His skill with a cine-camera was noted by his employers, and from time to time he made publicity or instructional films for Ransomes. In 1935 he made a film of trolleybuses being built at Orwell Works, some for Ipswich Corporation and others for export to Singapore and elsewhere.

He played an active part in the Ipswich Film Society, and made an amusing little film parodying their activities. On his return from war service in the RAF he was given a new job at Ransomes as a full-time film producer, work that enabled him to indulge his passion for travel. He filmed a Ransomes lawn-mower cutting the lawns of the Raffles Hotel in Singapore, ploughs breaking the soil in Australia and harvesters in use in Spain. He also developed a passion for archaeology, photographing excavations by the Suffolk Archaeological Unit as well as visiting Ur on the Euphrates and many another ancient city.

With the formation of the Ipswich Society in the 1960s, when it seemed likely that the town would be swamped by forced expansion that would double its population, Don found yet another outlet for his energies. Many of his films were put together for showing at meetings of the society, one being a special compilation to celebrate the society's twenty-first anniversary.

When Don died suddenly in 1992, his films were given to the East Anglian Film Archive, which organised some very successful showings at the Ipswich Film Theatre. The EAFA has since issued two compilations on videotape, *Don Chipperfield's Ipswich* and *Do you remember? Ipswich*.
☛ **See also Ransomes, Sims & Jefferies**

CHRISTCHURCH MANSION

Following the suppression of the Priory of Holy Trinity or Christchurch in 1536, its site was sold in 1545 to Paul Withypoll, a London merchant whose wife was a member of the Curzon family of Brightwell. Two years later their son Edmund inherited the property and began building a brick mansion there;

Christchurch Mansion, once the home of the nobility, had become a museum by the time this photograph was taken in the early years of the twentieth century.

when the Catholic Mary came to the throne various people found opportunity to attack him over his allegedly high-handed attitude, though his grave slab claimed he died without an enemy. In 1645 Elizabeth Withypoll married Leicester Devereux, who four years later inherited the title 6th Viscount Hereford; he made a number of alterations to the house and estate. When the Fonnereaus acquired the estate in 1735, they stocked the park with deer and opened up the area at the front of the house, which until then had consisted of a series of courtyards. The last Fonnereau to live at Christchurch Mansion was William Neale Fonnereau, who in 1892 offered the estate to the corporation for £50,000. The ratepayers voted against purchase and the land was bought by a property syndicate, which sold off part of it for building. Felix Thornley Cobbold, a member of the syndicate, then presented the mansion to the town as a gift on condition that the corporation purchase the rest of the park, which it did in 1895. The mansion was later opened as a museum.

CHURCHES, LOST

At the time of Domesday Book there were at least eleven churches within the borough. The Conqueror's survey of 1086 does not mention St Mildred's, which stood on the Cornhill, and its omission suggests that the list is incomplete. It includes Holy Trinity, which stood somewhere on the site of Christchurch Mansion; St Augustine, south of the river within a half-mile of Stoke Bridge, whose parish was absorbed by St Peter's; and St Michael, which has disappeared so completely that its site is unknown.

The church of Osterbolt, which stood somewhere between Fore Street and Shire Hall Yard, seems to have disappeared in the fourteenth century. All Saints, which may have stood on a triangular site at the junction of Handford Road and London Road, has also been lost, but some carved stones from this church were incorporated into St Nicholas's Church in the fourteenth or fifteenth century; by 1383 the parish had been absorbed by St Matthew's.

Also outside the town bank was St George's Chapel, from which the present George Street took its name. This ceased to be used for worship some time in the mid-sixteenth century, and was then used as a barn, at least until 1764 when its hay and corn were set alight accidentally through a boy at a funeral knocking his blazing torch against the fence. It was in those days customary to hold funerals by torchlight but, as a result of the burning of the former chapel, it was recommended that the custom should be abolished.
☞ *See also St Mildred's*

CIVIC CENTRE

Having outgrown the Town Hall, the borough council embarked on an ambitious scheme to build a Civic Centre on the edge of the town's shopping area. This new local government focus was meant to match the new road system, which was to be the first major amendment to the Saxon street layout. The first element, completed in 1967, was a spiral underground car park, the first in Britain and only the second in Europe; it cost £362,000. The Civic Centre itself, a tower block built to house all the departments of the borough council and to be the powerhouse of local government in Ipswich, opened in 1971. The third element was the new police station in Elm Street, together with the courts buildings. Unfortunately, the Civic Centre is likely to be abandoned by Ipswich Borough Council because, little more than thirty years after its opening, it is in so poor a state that the cost of renovation exceeds the cost of moving to other premises.

CIVIC DRIVE
Part of a grand scheme in the 1960s to take traffic away from the town centre, Civic Drive is a dual carriageway running from the St Matthew's roundabout at the foot of Berners Street to a large roundabout at Greyfriars, from where Franciscan Way was to have continued along the line of Cromwell Street and across Brook Street to Fore Street. The Civic Centre, a spiral underground car park, the police station and two large office blocks (for what was at the time of building the Eagle Star insurance company) were built alongside the new road.
☛ *See also Franciscan Way*

CLARKSON STREET
Like several other streets north of Handford Road laid out on land owned by the Alexander family, Clarkson Street is named after one of the stalwarts of the anti-slavery campaign. Thomas Clarkson was born in Wisbech in 1760, the son of the master of the Free Grammar School there. He devoted his life to the abolition of slavery, after writing a prize-winning dissertation on the slave trade while at Cambridge. One of the founders of the Anti-Slavery Society, and joint vice-president with William Wilberforce, Clarkson lived at Playford Hall, north-east of Ipswich, and was on friendly terms with many of the leading local Quakers who supported his campaign. He died there in 1846, having seen the abolition of the slave trade in 1803 and emancipation of the slaves thirty years later.

CLAY LANE
This lane ran outside the town bank from St Matthew's Street to Rotten Row; today it is known as Crown Street. In fact the singularly descriptive name may not have alluded to its miry condition but could have derived from Albricius dil Cley, a fourteenth-century bigwig, or even from the earlier Thurstan de Cley. Earlier it was known simply as 'the highway from the Old Barregates to the New Barregates', that is, from the North Gate to the West Gate.
☛ *See also Steelyards*

CLENCH, JUDGE JOHN

The first known Recorder of Ipswich, appointed in 1573, Judge Clench was the son of John Clench of Wethersfield in Essex and his wife. He was admitted as a student at Lincoln's Inn on 11 February 1556 and was called to the bar in 1568, being appointed a judge in 1580. Settling in Holbrook, he bought from Ipswich Corporation land and properties in that parish which had been left by Edmund Daundy in 1515 so the bailiffs could pay the friars a sum each year to pray for him and his relatives. Judge Clench is said to have been a favourite with Queen Elizabeth I, but he received no honours from her. In 1600 he was excused attendance at court because of his age and infirmities, and in 1603 was granted a pension; he died in 1607 and was buried in Holbrook Church, where there is a massive memorial to him.

CLIFF BREWERY

For over 250 years, from 1746, beer was brewed at the Cliff, where water from the Holywells estate ran down to the Orwell. It was the water – 'liquor' to the brewer – that attracted Thomas Cobbold to the site. He had spent twenty years brewing at Harwich with the increasingly brackish local water, and with water carried over the Stour from a spring at Erwarton, before moving to Ipswich in 1743; three years later, he built the brewery at the Cliff. His son, also Thomas, took over when Thomas Cobbold died in 1752, and in turn his son John continued the family businesses, which included malting as well as brewing, and also the buying and selling of corn and coal, plus banking and shipowning. Later generations got involved with railways and politics, and proved remarkable benefactors to the town.

In the 1890s, the old brewery was proving inadequate, and the Cobbolds called in a specialist architect, William Bradford, to design a new brewery embodying all the latest principles. It was built on the site of the old one in 1894–6. Among its state-of-the-art equipment was a horizontal steam engine, built no more than half a mile or so away by E.R. & F. Turner, at St Peter's Ironworks between the riverside and College Street. The brewery was extended in 1904, and again later in the twentieth century.

In 1957, the Cobbold enterprise merged with that of the Tollemache family and it was decided to concentrate brewing at the Cliff Brewery. A three-year enlargement of the brewery followed, and production at the Tollemache brewery, on a backland site between Carr Street and Tacket Street and to the east of Upper Brook Street, came to an end in 1961. The two families ran Tolly Cobbold until in 1977 the brewery and business were taken over by the Ellerman shipping group. Six years later this was sold to David and Frederick Barclay, and before long the brewery changed hands again and became part of the Brent Walker leisure group, headed by former boxer George Walker.

In 1989, it was announced that the brewery was to be closed and Tolly Cobbold ales were to be brewed in Hartlepool; it seemed the brewery would be demolished and the site sold for development. After Ipswich Borough Council had failed to persuade George Walker to reconsider, the brewery was listed as a building of historic and architectural interest. The listing included equipment such as a 1723-vintage copper and the Turner steam engine. A management buy-out by Brian Cowie and Bob Wales was successful, and the Cliff Brewery resumed production in 1991. It also became a brewery museum, with parties sampling the brew at the end of their tour. A special beer was brewed each year, and in the 1995 publicity joint managing director Brian Cowie impersonated Cardinal Wolsey in front of Wolsey's gate. It was a brave attempt to retain brewing in Ipswich, but alas it did not quite succeed. An amalgamation with Ridley's brewery at Hertford End, near Chelmsford, has meant the final closure of the Cliff Brewery.

☛ *See also Cobbold, John; Cobbold, Thomas*

CLIFF QUAY

The outbreak of war in 1914 put a stop to an ambitious scheme for the Wet Dock that included a large new entrance lock. When peace returned, the scheme was abandoned because of greatly increased costs of materials and labour. Instead, the Dock Commission acquired some fifty acres of Greenwich Farm to build a new quay with deep-water berths for ships too big to enter the dock. Construction of the new Cliff Quay began in 1923 and the first section, 600ft (183m) long, was opened two years later. A second length of quay was completed in 1929 and a third in 1938; a fourth stage – 1,450ft (442m) long – was finished in 1957, and the quay has since been extended to take in the site of the Cliff Quay power station.

☛ *See also **Bunting, HMS; Dock Commissioners; Wet Dock***

CLOCKMAKING

An eighteenth-century writer told of 'The Ingenious Mr. Moore, whose Clock and other Curiosities all the World has seen, and wondered at'. That particular clock is possibly the one advertised in the *Ipswich Journal* in 1720:

> This is to acquaint the Curious. That at the Great White Horse in Ipswich, is to be seen Tho. Moore's most famous Astronomical and Musical CLOCK, with new Additions, and will continue to be shown till the 16th of January next, at any Time of the Day, from nine in the Morning till eight at Night; during the Christmas holiday he showeth to Servants and Young People, if a Company, at Three-pence each.

Thomas Moore was also the inventor of a fusee watch that could be wound in either direction. He advertised its advantages in 1729:

St Margaret's Church in 1865, with the clock made by Thomas Moore in 1778. The early-fifteenth-century tower was transformed in 1871 when the upper part was rebuilt in a much more elegant fashion; the clock survived.

Whereas THOMAS MOORE, Clock and Watch Maker in Ipswich, have for many years observed the Misfortunes which very frequently happens to Pocket Watches of all sorts by sometimes coming into unskillful Hands, etc. and into the Hand of Servants (in the absence of the Owners thereof) they endeavouring to wind up the watch have turn'd the wrong way, and by doing so have broke the Work (and the like often happens, when the Juice of Grape predominate). Therefore, this is to give Notice, That the above Thomas Moore have now made up several curious Silver and Gold Watches (and will continue so to do) so curiously contriv'd that let the Watch be wound which way they please, either to Right or Left, they cannot fail of winding up the Watch.

The Moore family contributed several generations of clock and watchmakers in Ipswich, and so did the Cole family, who at one time had a shop on Cornhill, on the King Street corner (seen in page 48).

See Arthur Haggar and Leonard Miller, *Suffolk Clocks and Clockmakers* (British Horological Society, 1975)

CLOUTING, ARTHUR
The town's first Labour Mayor, Mr Clouting was employed at Ransomes, Sims & Jefferies. He it was who greeted the Prince of Wales when he arrived on 26 June 1930 to open Ipswich Airport and accompanied him on a visit to Ransomes' Orwell Works.
☛ *See also Airport*

COBBOLD, JOHN (1746–1835)

One of the third generation of Ipswich Cobbolds, John took over the family businesses in brewing, shipowning and banking. He built the Holywells mansion overlooking the springs which had given rise to the brewery at The Cliff, and it was his strawberry roan horse that was stolen by Margaret Catchpole and ridden to London. His eldest son, also named John (1774–1860), took a leading part in bringing the railway to Ipswich. The younger John married one of the Chevallier family from Aspall, the family that gave its name to a fine malting barley said to have had its origin in an ear of barley that a farmworker discovered in his boot after a day's threshing.

☛ *See also Cliff Brewery*

John Chevallier Cobbold.

COBBOLD, JOHN CHEVALLIER (1797–1882)

The eldest son of the second John Cobbold (1774–1860) was involved with his father in the formation of the Eastern Union Railway and represented Ipswich in Parliament for 20 years. He also took a leading part in the planning of the Wet Dock and became one of the Dock Commissioners. Appropriately, he was Mayor of Ipswich in 1842, the year the dock was opened; he sailed out through the new lock on a little sloop, the *Director*, on the opening day. He was eulogised by a writer in the *Suffolk Mercury* as being 'so closely mixed up with the social and public life of the town as to be inseparable from the actual identity of Ipswich'.

☛ *See also Cliff Brewery; Dock Commissioners; Railway, Eastern Union; Wet Dock*

COBBOLD, THE REVEREND RICHARD

A son of the first John Cobbold, Richard is best known as a Victorian novelist and as the author of *The History of Margaret Catchpole*, said to be 'the best read book in Ipswich, if not in Suffolk'. In 1859 he wrote a letter to the *Suffolk Chronicle* claiming that Margaret Catchpole was on a visit to Ipswich. 'Yes, sir, she was in the train with me,' he told the editor. 'Margaret Catchpole is upon a visit to Mr. Roe's in Brook Street in your town … perhaps some who remember her may like to see her.' The people of Ipswich duly rose to the bait, and Owen Roe's shop at 2 Upper Brook Street was besieged by the curious. All they saw was a somewhat imaginative painting of Margaret by her 'biographer' in the shop window. Doubtless Mr Owen Roe, looking-glass manufacturer, carver, gilder and picture-dealer – and the parson's brother-in-law – benefited considerably from this shameless publicity stunt. Margaret Catchpole had in fact died in 1819.

On another occasion Richard Cobbold was out walking in Wortham, the parish of which he was rector for many years, when he came upon two chimney sweeps sitting beside the road enjoying their breakfast. While chatting, he remarked how much he envied their nice white teeth, which looked all the whiter against their sooty faces. Back came the quick retort from one that they would change teeth with him for a pound. Now the parson had a set of false teeth, something of a rarity in nineteenth-century Suffolk. He pretended to tug at his teeth and, after a good deal of apparent effort, pulled them out. The two sweeps were terrified by the sight; they jumped up and ran to the Queen's Head, calling to the landlady, Mrs. Mary Allen, 'Missus, give us some brandy – we've just seen the Devil!'

☛ *See also Catchpole, Margaret*

COBBOLD, THOMAS (1680–1752)

A member of a Suffolk family which had farmed in Rattlesden and Tostock in the sixteenth and seventeenth centuries, Thomas Cobbold set up a brewery in Harwich in 1723. Finding the Harwich water brackish, he brought pure water across the Stour in water schuyts from a spring at Erwarton. Then in 1746 he moved his brewery to Ipswich, to The Cliff close to the Holy Wells. A brewery operated there for more than 250 years, until 2003.

☛ *See also Cliff Brewery*

COCKFIGHTING

The natural aggression of cockerels was exploited by 'sportsmen' at least from the Middle Ages onwards, gamecocks being bred to be matched in fights to the death. To prevent the cocks taking flight their wings were clipped, and to aid their fighting prowess they had metal spurs strapped to their legs. Many an Ipswich hostelry had its cockpit on the premises. A new cockpit was built at the Bear and Crown in Westgate Street in 1752, and three years later the licensee, Edmund Orford, announced a main of cocks between the Gentlemen of Cambridgeshire and the Gentlemen of Norfolk and Suffolk on the two race days. Some years later the cockpit of the Cock and Pye in Upper Brook Street was the venue for another raceday main, it being announced that 'The Cocks will be pitted at 11 o'clock, and immediately after the Race is over'.

COFFEE HOUSE, THE OLD

Standing on the corner of Tavern Street and Tower Street used to be a mid-sixteenth-century timbered building with a wealth of fine carving on the timbers. It had a highly decorative corner-post with half-life-size figures of Faith, Hope and Charity surmounted by a grinning satyr on the ground floor and other figures on the upper storey. On the Tavern Street face, the cornice at eaves level bore the names of Henry and Dorcas Buckingham, who were apparently the owners at the beginning of the seventeenth century. John Glyde tells us in his book *Illustrations of Old Ipswich* (Ipswich, 1889) that Buckingham was admitted as a burgess in 1601, and that he was twice elected as a governor of Christ's Hospital. He was churchwarden of St Mary-le-Tower in 1608, when fiery Samuel Ward, the town preacher, was attracting great crowds to the church. He and his fellow-churchwarden, George Raymond, paid for a gallery to be built on the north side of the church to accommodate the overflow. In return, the churchwardens received seat-rents from those who were not parishioners of St Mary's.

Later in the sixteenth century when coffee taverns, at which customers could obtain coffee as well as the wines and other drinks available from the many inns, became popular this house was turned over to such purpose, first appearing in the parish rate books in this guise in 1689. In London Lloyd's coffee house became well known as the gathering place for shipowners and those who were prepared to insure their vessels and cargoes, and doubtless the Ipswich coffee house also numbered the maritime fraternity among its customers. When it was offered for sale in 1767 by its then owner, Josiah Harris, it was said to have coffee, tea, card and dining rooms, and was linked with the adjoining Assembly Room that had been built during the 1750s. It was bought by a number of shareholders who included the Reverend Richard Canning, the minister of St Lawrence's Church and the author of a book that aroused the fury of a section of the Corporation by revealing the way in which that body had misused and misapplied the various charities. The shareholders then leased the premises to Daniel Bamford, who apparently had considerable experience as a landlord. His experience did not prevent him from coming into conflict with the law in 1771–72, when he was convicted of allowing gaming in the coffee house and was disqualified by the magistrates from holding a victualling licence; he was guilty of having allowed his customers to play billiards! Bamford appealed against the conviction, and the Court of King's Bench allowed his appeal and quashed his conviction. Bamford later moved to the Great White Horse.

Alas, the wonderfully decorated front of the Old Coffee House became a victim of the changes that came over the town in the course of the nineteenth and twentieth centuries. The process of 'modernisation' began early in Ipswich, for between 1815 and 1818 the Great White Horse and other buildings on the north side of Tavern Street lost their ornate fronts when the eastern end of that street was widened. The jettied fronts of the old timber-framed houses were taken off and replaced by perpendicular new fronts of the fashionable white brick made in the brickyards of the Ipswich area. John Glyde writes scathingly of how 'so picturesque a specimen of domestic architecture' was torn off 'in order that a few inches of ground should be added to the footway!' The rest of the building survived into the twentieth

century, and then the whole was torn down to make way for premises occupied for many years by the British Home Stores; since BHS moved into the Buttermarket these premises have been taken over by Superdrug.
☞ *See also Assembly Rooms*

COLD DUNGHILLS

This area to the south of the suburb of St Helen's was used as the dumping ground for the town's sewage and refuse. In 1543 it was decreed that 'noe person shall lay any horsdung in any place within this Burrow and liberties thereof, nor any manner of muck or filthe uppon the Dikes, or nigh to the same, under forfaiture of 3d. eache skepfull, and 12d. each load; nevertheless, the sweeping of the streete may be laid on the common ground called Warwicks pitts'. The 'pitts' was the area later known as the Cold Dunghills. At the same time the town authorities gave orders for dealing with stray pigs, which were to be taken to a pound erected in the 'pitts'. There is a reminder of both sewage and strays in the late seventeenth century, when Ogilby names a lane on the line of the present-day Waterworks Street as Dunghill Pound Lane.
☞ *See also Ogilby, John*

COLEHILL

A name used until the seventeenth century for what is now Silent Street. It is sometimes confused with the Cold Dunghills, the dumping ground for the town's refuse and sewage, which was further east in the vicinity of what later became the Rope Walk.
☞ *See also Silent Street*

CO-OPERATIVE SOCIETY

What is now the Ipswich and Norwich Co-operative Society had its beginnings in 1867 as the Ipswich Industrial Co-operative Society, though it began trading only in a rented shop in Carr Street. The society is said to have begun with only 114 members and capital of just £80, and the early years were difficult. In 1875 the society bought the Wellington Inn and turned it into business premises; the old clubroom proved very suitable for members' meetings and for the educational part of the society's activities at that period. Over the years the former Wellington disappeared beneath new premises with a considerable frontage in Carr Street, and branches were established in outlying parts of Ipswich and nearby towns and villages. The society's education programme has developed alongside the business and from children's dancing classes were born the Co-op Juniors, whose shows have been a feature of the Ipswich entertainment scene for more than half a century. Amalgamation with the Norwich society has resulted in a wide-ranging business which today bears no resemblance to the struggling little shop of 1868. In 2000 the society had a membership of 297,000 and annual turnover of £250 million.

Packard's original artificial fertiliser factory on the quay, with Coprolite Street running up to the left.

COPROLITE STREET

A short street running from Duke Street to the quay, Coprolite Street was formed in the 1850s at about the time that Edward Packard set up a fertiliser works using coprolites as its raw material. The works lay just to the south of Coprolite Street.

☞ *See also Coprolites*

COPROLITES

The phosphatic nodules known as coprolites were discovered at the foot of 'The Crag' in the coastal region of Suffolk about 1840. Professor J.S. Henslow identified them as being almost pure phosphate, and in 1843 Edward Packard, an agricultural chemist at Saxmundham, was grinding the nodules in a mill at Snape and dissolving the ground coprolites in sulphuric acid to produce an artificial fertiliser. Thus began the fertiliser industry that became so important in East Anglia in later years. By mid-century Edward Packard had set up a works in the dock area of Ipswich, and in 1854 he set up a superphosphate works at Bramford, claimed to be the first of its kind in Britain. Towards the end of the nineteenth century the supply of coprolites

The nameplate of Coprolite Street fixed to the 'white' brick wall of what had been Packard's fertiliser works.

dwindled, and phosphates were brought into the port of Ipswich from North Africa and elsewhere for the manure factories.

CORN EXCHANGE

Corn was bought and sold in the open on Cornhill for many centuries, but at the start of the nineteenth century it was decided that a special building ought to be provided where farmers and merchants could meet and do their business in more congenial conditions. The corn merchants and dealers agreed to pay an annual subscription for a stand, and the farmers also agreed to contribute. A purpose-built exchange was designed by George Gooding, who had earlier designed and built the unsuccessful Rotunda, and the first stone was laid by Edward Bacon, one of the bailiffs, in 1810. Above the entrance was erected the figure of Justice from the Market Cross, the sword and scales of Justice being exchanged for a sickle and a bundle of ears of wheat to turn her into Ceres. In 1830 G.R. Clarke remarked wryly that he was sorry 'to see that, at the present moment, this figure is without her sickle and wheat-ears; and it is difficult to know whether this goddess, thus divested of her attributes, may be considered as Flora, Astrea, or Ceres.' That was not all that had gone wrong, for the arrangement by which the merchants were to pay rent had been neglected and 'from mismanagement and misunderstanding … the Corn Exchange is … a heavy loss to the corporation'.

For all that it looked rather fine, this Corn Exchange was not a particularly good place for business as it had no roof, and there was little protection from the rain. In 1849 the corporation was asked to remedy this and complete

The figure of Justice from the Market Cross has been transmogrified into Ceres on the Corn Exchange, seen here in 1865. On the other side of what was then King Street is the shop of R.S. Cole, the watchmaker.

rebuilding took place: pictures of the new Corn Exchange show that it had one important accessory that the old one had lacked, a roof. This sufficed for thirty years, and then in 1879 the corporation bought the buildings on the King Street corner at the back of the Town Hall for the site of a new Corn Exchange; the old one made way for an imposing Post Office. From the 15 designs submitted, the corporation chose that by Brightwen Binyon, a successful architect responsible for a number of other buildings in and around Ipswich, as well as public buildings throughout the country. The cornerstone of the building was laid with considerable ceremony on 22 October 1880, and the opening took place on 26 July 1882.

For ninety years the Corn Exchange played a vital part in the life of the town, being home to the provision market and also the venue for many public events as well as providing a place of business for merchants and farmers. Then in 1972–5 it was completely remodelled. In 1975, European Architectural Heritage Year, it was opened as an entertainment and arts centre by the Duke of Gloucester. It still fulfils that role, though there are plans to sell it off.

See R.L. Cross, *The Living Past – A Victorian Heritage* (Ipswich Borough Council, 1975)

CORNHILL

The ancient centre of Ipswich, the Cornhill was the place where corn brought in from the countryside was laid out for sale. It is possible that in early Anglo-Saxon times the Wuffinga Kings of East Anglia had a royal residence on the Cornhill alongside St Mildred's Church, which later became the town hall. In 1614 the Great Court decided to bring water to a conduit on the Cornhill. Later the same year it was announced that householders could take water from the conduit for a £5 fine, if they paid the fine within 21 days; those who came later would have to pay annual rents as well as fines.

☛ *See also Market Cross; St Mildred's Church; Town Hall*

A reminder of the not-too-far-off days when Cornhill was a busy traffic centre. The ornate Victorian buildings in this view were designed by architect Thomas William Cotman.

COTMAN, THOMAS WILLIAM (1847–1925)

Architect nephew of John Sell Cotman, he was born in Bermondsey. His family moved to Ipswich when he was still young and he trained at the Ipswich School of Art, setting up business in 1869. He left his mark on Ipswich, designing the Crown & Anchor Hotel in Westgate Street and buildings on Cornhill that were later cut through to form Lloyds Avenue, and even more on Felixstowe, where many of the houses were built in the 1890s and 1900s. With the Hon. Douglas Tollemache he designed the Felix Hotel at Felixstowe, originally to have been named The Balmoral.

COWELL, W.S

In 1818 Abraham Kersey Cowell, pastor of Walton Baptist Chapel, acquired the bookselling business of Richard Nottingham Rose in the Buttermarket at which his second son, Samuel Harrison Cowell, then 16, was an apprentice. His father engaged a 'competent and confidential person' to manage the firm until Samuel could take over. Eight years later Samuel acquired premises in Old Gaol Lane (later known as Old Market Lane) next door to his Buttermarket shop and there opened a tea, coffee and spice warehouse; he continued to expand the business until it occupied a large area between the Buttermarket shop and Falcon Street. In a directory of 1879 the firm was described as wholesale stationers, letterpress, anastatic and lithographic printers, machine rulers, account book and paper-bag manufacturers, and wholesale tea dealers. After Samuel died in 1875, the business was run by his son Walter Samuel Cowell and W.B. Hanson, who had joined the firm as manager in 1866, under the name W.S. Cowell, its name ever since it became a limited company in 1900. For many years the firm also had a wholesale and retail wines, spirits and cigar business in Old Market Lane and a rag and metal business in Falcon Street; in more recent years the shop on the corner of Buttermarket and Old Market Lane became a department store called Cowells Store Ltd.

COYTE'S GARDENS

The name of a byway between Friars Street and Princes Street, this is a reminder of one of the many splendid gardens that once existed in the town. When Joseph Pennington produced his map in 1778 spacious gardens laid out with paths among shrubberies occupied much of the built-up area; a few years earlier John Kirby had observed in the second edition of *The Suffolk Traveller* that 'one favourable Circumstance is almost peculiar to this Place, which is, that most of the better Houses, even in the Heart of the Town, have convenient Gardens adjoining to them, which make them more airy and healthy, as well as more pleasant and delightful'. The particular garden alluded to in the street name was the 'physick garden' started in 1721 by Dr

There is no trace of the physic garden to be found today in Coyte's Gardens, a minor stone-setted byway among the office blocks of modern Ipswich.

William Beeston (1671–1731) who was, according to Daniel Defoe, 'exquisitely skilled in botanick knowledge'. On Dr Beeston's death the garden passed to his nephew, Dr William Coyte (1708–1775), who gave his name to this byway.

CRANE

On the Common Quay, where all strangers coming by sea were required to unload, was a crane, first mentioned in the town records in 1477. It is not known whether loads were hoisted by a treadwheel like that in the famous Harwich Navy Yard crane (which survives from the 1660s) or whether some form of hand winch was employed. Orders were given in 1618 for the erection of 'a new crane and cranehouse', and another new crane was erected in 1727 when John Sparrowe and John Cornelius were bailiffs; it survived until the construction of the Wet Dock and can be seen in earlier pictures of the Common Quay.

☛ *See also* Wet Dock

CROMWELL SQUARE

Originally called Cromwell Street and lined with terrace houses, this rather short and insignificant street ran from St Nicholas Street to Friars Street and took its name from Thomas Cromwell, Cardinal Wolsey's right-hand man. It was to have disappeared when Franciscan Way was constructed, for this dual carriageway was to have continued eastwards from Greyfriars across St Nicholas Street and Lower Brook Street. Most of the houses were demolished to make way for the new road, only a Polish tailor who owned a house on the north side being stubborn enough to fight the compulsory purchase order. Eventually plans changed, the route was diverted into Greyfriars Road and a new Star Lane, and Cromwell Square survived to become a car park.

☛ *See also Franciscan Way*

CROYDON'S

A painting of Father Time by Henry Todd (1846–1898) for many years decorated the front wall of Croydon's shop at 50–52 Tavern Street, along with other painted panels recording the generations that had worn Croydon's wedding rings. The firm of Croydon & Sons, watchmakers, jewellers, goldsmiths and silversmiths, had been established in 1865 by Charles Harry Edward Croydon, who had served his apprenticeship with John Warren of the Buttermarket. It remained a family business until 1994, expanding into a number of other centres, including Norwich. An unwise diversification into shipping was partly responsible for the firm going into receivership in 1994, and the business was then acquired by a family firm from Lancashire, Preston & Duckworth of Bolton. In 2004 a decision was taken to move to smaller premises in the Buttermarket. The ornate Tavern Street shop – whose façade was modelled on the Ancient House – is not nearly as old as it looks, having been the result of a 1931 rebuilding.

A pre-Christmas view of Croydon's shop in Tavern Street, once a popular place for those seeking a special seasonal present, or a wedding ring.

CURSON, LORD

Robert Curson, born about 1460 at Blaxhall, was knighted in 1489 and appointed Sheriff of Norfolk and Suffolk seven years later. He seems to have had a remarkable career, for after being made captain of Hampnes Castle, near Calais, in 1499 he obtained leave from Henry VII to fight the Turks, in the army of the Holy Roman Emperor, Maximilian I. Very soon, spies reported that Curson was complaining to the emperor about Henry's tyranny in England and was seeking support for a Yorkist rebellion. He and five others were proclaimed traitors from the pulpit at St Paul's Cross in London in October 1501. Two of the five were beheaded and two were sent to the Tower of London, but Curson seems to have been pardoned, which suggests that he may have been acting as a double agent. In the next eight years he was pardoned three times more, which does indeed suggest that the king had reason to treat him differently from other men branded as traitors. Maximilian too regarded Curson with favour, since he made him a Count of the Holy Roman Empire. This title seems to have been recognised at the English court from about 1513, when as Lord Curson, Master of the Ordnance in the Rearward Column, he served under Charles Brandon, Duke of Suffolk, during the war in France. In 1520 he accompanied Henry VIII to the Field of the Cloth of Gold. When Lord Curson died in 1535 he was buried in the Greyfriars, under a magnificent tomb, which was later moved to St Peter's Church but has since disappeared.

CURSON'S HOUSE

The house in Silent Street that Lord Curson built as his residence about 1500 was a very fine one, with a 'strong and stately brick porch' which, G.R. Clarke tells us, projected a considerable way into the street. The porch was pulled down in 1760 and the main building survived only a little longer; it was said that the large and lofty rooms included a banqueting hall profusely ornamented with coats of arms of the Curson family. Cardinal Wolsey planned to take over this mansion as his Ipswich home, but Curson asked for three years' grace to find an alternative, and by then Wolsey had fallen from power and died.

When Thomas Manning, the former Prior of Butley, was made the first and only suffragan Bishop of Ipswich, the house became his residence; subsequently the house was granted to the bishops of Norwich, who used it when visiting the Suffolk part of their diocese. Bishop Matthew Wren stayed there in 1635 and set about dealing with the town's nonconforming ministers and churchwardens. His actions, and perhaps his very presence, provoked serious rioting which seems to have had the silent approval of the local authorities. The bishop was forced to flee, being hunted out of town by a mob of 'younge fellowes, disorderly men and diverse sorts of people gathered', but he got his revenge by proceeding against the town in the infamous Court of Star Chamber.

During the Dutch wars, later in the seventeenth century, the house was a hospital for sick and wounded naval seamen, and it was known thereafter as the King's Hospital. Later it became a public house with the sign of the Elephant and Castle. The slippery slope to dereliction continued when it was acquired by Robert Trotman, a maltster and six times bailiff; he seems to have converted the already ruinous building, or some part of it, into a malting.

☛ *See also King's Hospital; Silent Street*

CUSTOM HOUSE, OLD

The original Custom House, a sixteenth-century timber-framed building with a colonnaded walkway along the front, was taken down in 1843 to make way for a new one, following the opening of the dock. During his second term of office as mayor in 1840–41, Peter Bartholomew Long, clerk to the Dock Commissioners, commissioned a young architect named John Medland Clark to draw up plans for an imposing new building. The *Ipswich Journal* reported in April 1840 that the corporation had decided to pull down the Custom House, crane and warehouses on the Common Quay 'which in consequence of the dock works were comparatively of little value in their present state' and to replace them with 'a handsome building … capable of affording increased accommodation as a Custom House, sufficient warehouse and other rooms for the business of wharfingers, an Excise office, and a coffee-room for captains of vessels and others connected with the shipping of the port'. Nothing was done until in 1843 the corporation's Estate Committee decided to go ahead with the building of a 'Hall of Commerce'. The design was the subject of a competition and the winner, to nobody's surprise, was John Medland Clark. With four stone columns supporting a pediment with the borough arms, and a set of steps leading up to a first-floor entrance, the new Custom House was most imposing. It has a special place in architectural history, for it is an early example of the use of red brick for an important public building rather than the white bricks for which Suffolk brickyards are so well known. The Old Custom House, as it became known in the twentieth century, was the headquarters of the Ipswich Dock Commission, and the Ipswich Port Authority that succeeded it. Since Associated British Ports took over the port, the interior of the building, which had been divided up into smaller offices, has been restored to its original condition and the bonded store on the ground floor has been converted into a display and conference area. The doors of the cells that formed part of the police station at the back of the building are still to be seen, incorporated into the conference area.

☛ *See also Wet Dock*

DAIRY LANE

An earlier name of what is now Fonnereau Road.

☛ *See also Fonnereau Road*

DIESEL WORKS

Established in 1912 on land between Hadleigh Road and the River Gipping, the Diesel Works was set up by the British Diesel Company to produce the German-designed oil engines. The inventor, Dr Rudolf Diesel, disappeared from the SS *Dresden* on the night of 29–30 September 1913 as he was travelling to Harwich for a visit to the Ipswich works; his hat and neatly folded coat were found in the stern of the ship, but despite a search no trace could be found of the man himself. The works closed in 1914, but was reopened the following year by Vickers-Petter Ltd. who were producing large oil engines for submarines. The company also refitted Royal Navy submarines in Ipswich Dock; ten were overhauled during 1914, another twenty-six in 1916 and eighteen the following year. The works continued in production after the war under the name of Petters (Ipswich) Ltd but, with the Depression, production was transferred to Petters at Yeovil in 1928 and the works closed. A twin-cylinder two-stroke oil engine made at the Ipswich works is to be seen at Prickwillow Drainage Engine Museum; starting the engine involves heating the tops of the cylinders to cherry red with paraffin blowlamps, quite a spectacular process.

DOCK COMMISSIONERS

On 30 June 1837 the Ipswich Dock Act received Royal Assent from the young Queen Victoria. The new Dock Commissioners were to construct a dock in which ships could lie afloat at all states of the tide. The commissioners included John Cobbold and his son John Chevallier Cobbold, Jeremiah Head, shipbuilder William Bayley, attorney Peter Bartholomew Long, William Lane, the Collector of Customs for the port and a leading campaigner for the dock scheme, the banker Richard Dykes Alexander and other prominent townspeople. Although told by their engineer, Henry Palmer, that the dock should cost £58,100, the lowest tender submitted was one of some £65,000 from a David Thornbory, of King's Lynn. It was accepted by the Dock Commissioners in 1838, but this proved to be a mistake, because Thornbory cut corners and the commissioners had in the end to accept many extra bills. Thornbory seems to have been a wily customer: when he found himself in dispute with the commissioners, he had himself appointed one and thus became his own employer. With the dock completed in 1842, the Dock Commissioners went on to run the port for more than a century, eventually occupying the Old Custom House as their offices.

See Bob Malster & Bob Jones, *A Victorian Vision: The building of Ipswich Wet Dock* (Ipswich Port Authority, 1992)

☛ *See also River Commissioners; Wet Dock*

DOG'S HEAD STREET

The name of a street running from the Old Cattle Market to the junction with Upper and Lower Brook Street and Tacket Street, said to be derived from a hostelry with the sign of the Dog's Head in the Pot, which stood on the Brook Street corner in the seventeenth century; it was Dog's Head in Pot Lane in 1694. The Headboroughs' Book in 1686 has a reference to 'The signpost standing in the King's ground at the Dogs Head in the Pot shall pay annually one shilling petty rent'. A later name for the same hostelry seems to have been the White Hart and Punchbowl.

DOWNHAM BRIDGE

Not a bridge at all as it is understood today, Downham Bridge is a former ford with a hard bottom that crosses the River Orwell from near Pond Hall to Wherstead Strand. The hard bottom might be man-made paving, but there are some who believe it to be a natural formation. In the eighteenth century, large ships were too deep to get over the Downham Bridge ford even at high water and it was necessary to unload them into lighters, which brought the cargo up to Ipswich quays. It has been said that the ford is a Roman one carrying a direct road from Walton Castle to Colchester; what might be another road from Walton appears to pass through the town on its way to Combretovium, a Roman settlement and military station at Coddenham/Baylham, which was a focal point of the Roman road layout in the area. A Roman water control structure of some kind at this point has been suggested, but again there is no evidence to support this theory.

☛ *See Orwell, River*

DRAGLINES
☛ *See Ransomes & Rapier*

DUCK STREET

An old name for what is today known as Duke Street. This old name is found on both Ogilby's map of 1674 and Pennington's a hundred years later.
☛ *See also Ogilby, John; Pennington, Joseph*

EAST ANGLIAN DAILY TIMES

The first issue of the Ipswich-based daily newspaper appeared on Tuesday 13 October 1874, with Frederick Wilson (later Sir Frederick) as its first editor and Thomas Elkington in charge of commercial operations. The financial backing came from James Jeremiah Colman, the mustard king, who had also been behind the launching of the *Eastern Counties Daily Press* in Norwich four years earlier. In its early days the *East Anglian Daily Times* suffered severe opposition from the Tory *Ipswich Journal*, which claimed to be the first daily paper in Suffolk on the strength of having published daily for just one week in 1867, after which it reverted to weekly publication. For many years the Carr Street office of the *EADT*, with its distinctive corner turret,

was a prominent feature of the street until the company moved to Lower Brook Street in 1966. The *EADT* is now part of the Archant group.
☞ *See also* **Evening Star; Ipswich Journal**

EAST GATE
It is assumed that this stood at the end of Stepples Street (now Tacket Street and Orwell Place) at or near the junction with the Wash. In spite of the name Eastgates given to the Carr Street shopping precinct, the East Gate did not stand at the end of Carr Street, which apparently was blocked when the town rampart was thrown up. Those wishing to proceed out of town from Carr Street then had to divert down Cox Lane to reach the East Gate. There was an Osterbolt Church somewhere between Fore Street and Shire Hall Yard, whose name is thought to refer to this gate; it disappeared in the fourteenth century. No-one knows when the East Gate was demolished.
☞ *See also* **Bull Gate; North Gate; Walls, Town; West Gate**

EASTGATES CENTRE
This began life as the Carr Street Shopping Precinct. It was doubtless hoped that the new, somewhat imaginative name would remedy the initial lack of success in attracting shoppers.
☞ *See also* **Carr Street; East Gate**

The interior of the Eastgates shopping centre in Carr Street.

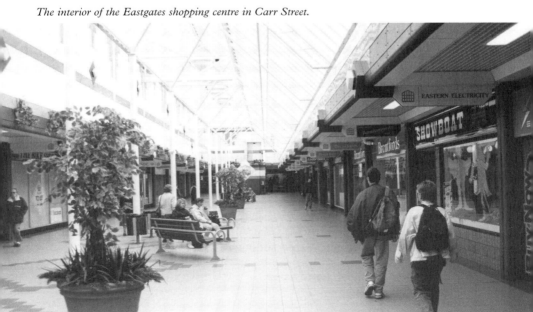

EGERTON, REGINALD

The son of a Norfolk rector, Reggie Egerton was a pioneer of the motor industry and saw a future for the motor vehicle when most people regarded it as a dangerous and pestilential novelty that would have its day and die. About 1902 he joined with the Botwoods to form Botwood & Egerton, motor engineers. Notorious for his many clashes with the law, Reggie promoted the car by long-distance trials, and he and a companion endeavoured to drive from John O'Groats to Lands End. Though atrocious weather prevented him from achieving his goal, he drove about 870 miles and 'traversed every kind of road in every kind of condition, experiencing every sort of weather, except thunder'. In 1904 Reggie was convicted by Ipswich Magistrates of driving in a manner dangerous to the public in Princes Street; he appealed and the Recorder quashed the conviction. It was widely claimed in the motoring press that it was the first successful appeal against the new Motor Car Act. His many convictions led *The Motor* in 1905 to refer to 'Mr Egerton of Ipswich, who has been the object of persistent irritation by the police in the town'. In 1910 Egerton left the Botwood enterprise and set up his own company, Egertons (Ipswich) Ltd in Northgate Street, opening new premises in Crown Street in 1928. Reggie's brother Hubert went into partnership with Gerard Mann, an electrical engineer, to form the Norwich firm of Mann, Egerton, which in 1919 took over the majority of shares in Botwood's.

See John F. Bridges, *Early Country Motoring* (1995)
☛ *See also Botwood's*

EMPRESS SKATING RINK

This roller-skating rink, with its tea gardens and pleasure grounds, stood on the corner of Portman Road and Portman Walk in the early years of the twentieth century. The product of a fashion for skating, it did not have a long existence.

ERNLEIGH ROAD

A residential road between Britannia Road and Goring Road, Ernleigh Road was laid out in the 1930s by Ernest Leigh, builder, plumber and decorator, who gave his name to it. He later built Halliwell Road, further along Britannia Road, which he named after his residence, Halliwell, 29 Cauldwell Hall Road.

EVENING STAR

When an Ipswich evening newspaper was launched by the *East Anglian Daily Times* in 1884 it was named *The Star of the East*, a title later shortened to *Evening Star*. The rival *Ipswich Journal* fought back by introducing the *Ipswich Herald*, but this was incorporated into its rival in 1898. The *Evening Star* is now a member of the Archant group.

EXECUTIONS

Between 1801 and 1920, thirty-eight men and seven women were executed at Ipswich Gaol. The first, W. Baldwin, a soldier, was hanged on 15 August 1801 for highway robbery; the last, a tram conductor, F.W. Storey, was executed on 16 June 1920 for the murder of a woman who had been a wartime 'clippie' on the trams. Until 1863 the hangings were carried out in public above the front of the prison, sometimes in the presence of large crowds of spectators; the last public execution was that of John Ducker, who had been convicted of murder, on 14 April 1863.

FA CUP

The national newspapers were incredulous when Ipswich Town FC not only played their way into the semi-final for the Football Association Cup in 1978 but beat mighty Millwall 6–1 on their own ground. This team – from 'a little East Anglian market town', as some sports writers described Ipswich (for the most part they penetrated no further than the Sporting Farmer in Princes Street) – was given little chance by the pundits, but the team was followed to Wembley by trainloads of Blues fans hoping to see Mick Mills and his men triumphant. It was the Town's first excursion to Wembley; their opponents, Arsenal – 'not so much a football club, more an institution' according to the official match programme – had won the Cup first in 1930 and had taken it back to Highbury three times more, in 1936, 1950 and 1971.

Watched by chairman Patrick Cobbold, his brother and former chairman John and their mother, Lady Blanche Cobbold, the Blues beat Arsenal by the only goal of the match, scored by midfielder Roger Osborne. Celebrations culminated in the team riding through Ipswich in an open-top bus, with captain Mick Mills holding the FA Cup aloft in triumph.

☛ *See also Football Club, Ipswich Town*

FELAW, RICHARD

A leading local merchant during the Wars of the Roses, Richard Felaw was a Yorkist sympathiser. He acted as local agent for Sir John Howard of Stoke-by-Nayland, who served as vice-admiral for Norfolk and Suffolk and was 'furnishing forth ships for the wars' with France that began in 1468. The Patent Rolls reveal Felaw's activities on behalf of the Crown during the reign of Edward IV, who came to the throne in 1461 after defeating the Lancastrians at Mortimer's Cross and Towton. Felaw and three other men were in 1461 appointed to provide wheat, malt, mutton, fish, salt and other things required for victualling the king's ships, and in June that year he was among the commissioners who had to provide six ships with 700 men-at-arms and archers for use against the king's French and Scottish enemies.

Three years later Felaw was one of the men appointed to assist the Duke of Norfolk in an inquiry into Lancastrian activities in East Anglia.

It is possible that Felaw took care of Sir John's son Thomas when he attended the Ipswich grammar school, to which Felaw left his house in St Edmund Pountney Lane (now Foundation Street) on his death in 1482/3. The Howard accounts for 1462–9 throw considerable light on Felaw's work with Sir John, who in 1463 visited 'Richard Felawys howse' and in 1466 'did recken with Herman berebrewer of Yipswyche' at Felaw's home. The accounts also describe Felaw's lading of the *Mary Talbot* of Lynn, on Sir John's instructions; among other things he supplied corn, hides, tallow, iron, salt and beer.

Felaw was eight times bailiff and twice the town's representative in Parliament. While a Member of Parliament in 1449, Felaw served on a commission of inquiry into the evasion of customs duties, and about 1458 he became Comptroller of Customs and Subsidies for the port, keeping account of customs duties paid by vessels entering and leaving the Orwell.
☛ *See also Felaw's House; Grammar School*

FELAW'S HOUSE
The house which Richard Felaw bequeathed to the grammar school on his death in 1482/3 no longer exists; it was demolished under the slum clearance programme in 1963 and the site is now occupied by a multi-storey car park.
☛ *See also Felaw, Richard; Grammar School*

FONNEREAU ROAD
The road that runs along the western side of Christchurch Park is named after the family that owned the estate for some 150 years. Originally the lower part of the road was known as Dairy Lane. The road was laid out and named Fonnereau Road about 1850 when development of the west side began; the estate was sold in 1894 to a property syndicate, which resold part of the park and building then began on the other side.
☛ *See also Dairy Lane*

FOOTBALL CLUB, IPSWICH TOWN
The story of Ipswich Town FC goes back to 1878. It was then known as Ipswich Association Football Club to distinguish it from the local rugby club, which had its home ground at Portman Road. The new club used the Inkerman as its headquarters and played on a pitch at Brook's Hall, on the opposite side of Norwich Road. With the formation of the Suffolk County FA in 1885, Ipswich Town appeared in the first two finals of the Suffolk Senior Cup, losing 3–1 to Woodbridge after two replays in 1886 and winning the trophy in 1887, beating Ipswich School 2–1. The club moved to Portman

F.S. MILLS SEC'C T FENN . BUGG   RUSHBROOKE CULLINGFORD E HARBORD A LIFFEN
W GARNHAM CAP. IPSWICH TOWN 1912 1913   REFEREE M'S S KILBRY
BAILEY LINESMAN W GREEN   DURRELL R.F BARLOW W.LEATHERS

The Ipswich Town team of 1912-13 in their blue and white striped shirts. The Blues did not become a professional side until 1936.

Road in 1888, at first sharing the ground with the rugby club; it is said that some team members played rugby on a Wednesday and soccer on the Saturday. In the 1930s supporters wanted better football, and in 1936 a meeting called for a professional side. The club was at first unwilling to change its status and so plans were laid to form an Ipswich United FC to field a professional team. Captain Ivan Cobbold, president of Ipswich Town FC, spoke out in favour of a professional club, and a week later Ipswich Town and the proposed Ipswich United merged to form Ipswich Town FC Ltd, with Captain Cobbold as chairman. The professional club won the Southern League Championship at its first attempt and then, only two years after its formation, was elected to the Third Division South. Much of the club's early success was due to the first managers, Mike O'Brien and Scott Duncan; the latter was manager from late in 1937 until 1955, when he handed over to a former Tottenham Hotspurs and England full-back with no managerial experience, Alf Ramsey. Manager no. 3 took the Town to the top of the First Division at their first attempt in 1962, and went on to be knighted for his work as national team manager after England won the World Cup. His successor, Bobby Robson, also later knighted, spent his first three years fighting against relegation, but in 1978 Ipswich Town won its way to the final of the FA Cup. Against the odds, the Blues beat Arsenal by a single goal, scored by midfielder Roger Osborne, to win the Cup. And in 1981 they topped that by winning the UEFA Cup.

☞ *See also FA Cup*

FOOTMAN, PRETTY & CO

It is said that Robert Footman established his linen drapers and silk mercers business in the Buttermarket on 21 June 1815, just three days after the Battle of Waterloo. He was soon joined by his brother John, who took over when

A view of Westgate Street from Cornhill in 1859 showing the imposing new Waterloo House to which John Footman & Co had moved in 1842.

Robert died at the early age of thirty-one. He moved to premises – which he named Waterloo House – on the Cornhill, next to Mumford's Passage, an alleyway long gone. John Footman was later joined by William Pretty and then Alexander Nicholson, and in 1842 the firm of John Footman & Co moved to Westgate Street and a new Waterloo House; the old building became Old Waterloo House. The Griffin Inn,

Old Waterloo House when it was occupied by James Beart's general drapery and costume warehouse. Mumford's Passage runs in a tunnel under the building behind the lamppost.

whose yard had been a venue for plays and entertainments, was demolished to make way for the new shop. John Footman died in 1854 and was buried in the churchyard of St Matthew's. By the 1870s the firm had become Footman, Pretty & Nicholson, wholesale and retail drapers, silk mercers, linen, manchester and carpet warehousemen, funeral furnishers, sewing machine agents and stay manufacturers. By the end of the century the name Nicholson had been dropped and the firm remained Footman, Pretty & Co. until a takeover by a national chain. After a major rebuilding of the store in 1981, the name was changed to Debenhams, but for many Ipswich people it is still 'Footmans'.

☛ *See also Pretty, William, & Sons; Staymakers*

FRANCISCAN WAY

Taking its name from the medieval Greyfriars, Franciscan Way was part of a 1960s plan for an inner ring road to take traffic clear of the centre. It was to run across St Nicholas Street and Lower Brook Street, cutting a swathe through one of the oldest parts of the town and causing the loss of some of the town's best old buildings, some timber-framed, but in the end a new single-carriageway road was built on the line of Greyfriars Road to a roundabout beside St Peter's Church. Another new road on the line of Star Lane carried traffic on across Fore Street and round behind St Clement's Church and then by way of Grimwade Street into the eastern part of Fore Street.

☛ *See also Civic Drive; Cromwell Square*

FRASER, R.D. & J.B

One of the town's longest-surviving businesses, Frasers is said to have been set up in 1833 by Roderick Donald Fraser in Elm Street. Fraser was a pawnbroker, who would lend money on the security of anything from a wedding ring or a piece of jewellery to a working man's Sunday suit; in 1844 he was one of five such tradesmen in the town. Pawnbrokers naturally acquired some expertise in the more valuable goods that were left as security, since they might have to sell them if, as quite often happened, the owners failed to pay up and reclaim their property; Donald Fraser styled himself pawnbroker, silversmith, clothier and general salesman. He was in due course joined by Joseph Brownsmith Fraser, and by 1879 the two men were in partnership. Their trade grew and they moved from Elm Street to extensive premises on Princes Street and Museum Street, which were destroyed in 1912 in a disastrous fire that spread to a number of nearby properties; they also had a furniture depository between Curriers Lane and Tanners Lane. Their distinctive shop was rebuilt after the fire and the firm continued to trade, latterly as Frasers (Ipswich) Ltd, as house furnishers, upholsterers and jewellers; they also had a cabinet and bedding works in Elm Street and auction rooms and depositories in Princes Street. About 1960 the firm was taken over by a large London furnishers and became Frasers (Maple) Ltd, but the firm closed down in 1984 and the shop building has since become offices.

FREEHOLD LAND SOCIETY, IPSWICH & SUFFOLK

Still in existence – now the Ipswich Building Society – this was set up in 1849 to provide a means of giving working men the vote. The middle classes had been enfranchised by the Reform Act of 1832, but not the ordinary worker. To quote the prospectus issued on 1 December 1849, the society aimed to improve the social position and promote the moral elevation of the unenfranchised population, by encouraging working people to invest their small savings, the accumulated money being used to purchase estates that could be divided into plots large enough to confer on their owners what was known as the forty-shilling suffrage: anyone owning a freehold worth at least forty shillings (£2) a year was entitled to a vote.

The letters FLS appear on the name-stones of many houses built by the Ipswich and Suffolk Freehold Land Society in the town.

The first property acquired was the Cauldwell Hall estate, between Woodbridge Road and Foxhall Road. It was divided into 282 allotments and

The characteristic offices of the Ipswich and Suffolk Freehold Land Society, now the Ipswich Building Society, on the corner of Upper Brook Street and Dogs Head Street, seen from Tacket Street before the demolition of the old shops on the opposite corner.

members had a ballot for the right to pay £23 and become freeholders. At the time the society had no power to purchase land, so the estate was bought by John Footman, a draper, William Dillwyn Sims, a partner in Ransomes & Sims, and William Fraser, a woollen draper, on the society's behalf.

Having sold the 282 Cauldwell Hall plots at a small profit, the society bought more land, in Ipswich, Bury St Edmunds, Stutton and Wickham Market. Towards the end of the century, the society helped develop Felixstowe, which received a boost in 1891 when the Empress of Germany, a daughter of Queen Victoria, chose to stay there with her children while the emperor was on an official visit to Britain.

From 1866 the Freehold Land Society operated as a building society, constructing houses and then selling them to members selected by ballot. The first such houses were the 'pretty and substantial six-room cottages' in Palmerston Road and Lancaster Road, off St Helen's Street in Ipswich. Those houses sold for £145 in 1866, and by 1878 some were selling for £180; property prices were rising even then. There are today many 'desirable properties' in Ipswich and elsewhere that bear the initials 'FLS' on a stone in the front wall.

☛ *See also California*

FREEHOLD ROAD

The spine road of the Cauldwell Hall estate, laid out in the mid-nineteenth century by the Freehold Land Society, which gave the road its name. This body purchased the land and sold plots to working people, with the intention they would thereby become eligible to vote.

☛ *See also California; Freehold Land Society, Ipswich & Suffolk*

FREEMEN

When King John gave Ipswich its charter in 1200, he granted it 'to the Burgesses of Ipswich, Our Borough of Ipswich, with all its Appurtenances and Liberties, and all its free Customs'. The burgesses were the free men of the town, those who had gained their freedom by service (by having completed an apprenticeship with a burgess), by purchase or in some other way. They had many privileges, the main one being the right to trade in the town without paying for doing so; and they also had duties, one of which was to pay towards the costs of their local government. In time the word burgess was replaced by the term freeman. Another privilege of the freemen was that of voting for the borough's members of Parliament; in the eighteenth and early nineteenth centuries this right could be sold to the highest bidder, and frequently was.

The freedom is passed down from father to son, and since 1990 in Ipswich also to daughters. There is a Guild of Ipswich Freemen, and those who have sworn an oath of loyalty to the Mayor and have taken up their freedom are intensely proud of their heritage.

☛ *See also Bailiffs; Charter; Portmen*

FRESTON TOWER

Built of red brick decorated with diapering in blue brick, Freston Tower overlooks the Orwell from the south bank not far below the town. Legend has it that the tower was built for the education of the beautiful Ellen de Freston, who each weekday studied a different subject on a different floor, starting with charity on the ground floor and continuing on to astronomy on the top floor. Another story tells how the tower was once part of a much larger building; the first three storeys have no windows on the south side, adding weight to this suggestion. There are good views down the Orwell, so perhaps it was built as a lookout by a merchant who wished to know as soon as possible when his ships were returning. Whatever its purpose, Freston Tower was probably built by Thomas Gooding, a well-to-do Ipswich mercer, a dealer in silk and fine textiles, who was out to impress. He acquired the lordship of the manor of Freston from Christopher Latimer in 1554. Tree-ring dating of beams in the first two storeys shows that the oak was felled in the spring of 1579. Queen Elizabeth visited Ipswich in 1579, and it is possible that she travelled by water; if she did, she could not have failed to notice Gooding's new tower, and it may be that the purpose of this folly was to impress the queen.

Following restoration, the tower now belongs to the Landmark Trust, which cares for unusual old buildings and lets them to people seeking an unusual setting for their holiday.

A nineteenth-century photograph of Freston Tower, pleasantly set amid parkland overlooking the Orwell.

GALLEY, THE IPSWICH

In 1294 Edward I ordered that twenty-six towns on the east and south coasts should between them provide a score of galleys for the French wars. Galleys were the maids-of-all-work of the navy in the thirteenth and fourteenth centuries, employed in convoy duty when impressed merchant ships were conveying English soldiers across the Channel, in stopping and searching ships at sea and in enforcing customs regulations. They were also used during the Hundred Years War (1336–1453) for cross-Channel raiding by both the English and the French.

Among the corporation records are the accounts for the building of a new galley and a barge for it, 'for the defence of the realm and the security of the seas against the enemies of King and kingdom, by the King's writ and by order of William de Marchia, Bishop of Bath and Wells, the King's Treasurer, on behalf of the King in his 23rd year [of his reign], under the inspection and taxation of Philip Harneys and Thomas Aylred, assigned to this work by the said writ'. Harneys and Aylred were prominent citizens, but there is no evidence that they were shipbuilders. Harneys is said to have been the second richest man in Ipswich in 1282. The cost of building the galley was £195 4s.11½d. and of the barge £23 7s.¼d., and accounts were rendered to the Exchequer by the bailiffs, John de Causton and John Lew.

The galley was then taken down the Orwell for its sea trials. Unfortunately the trials were interrupted by a storm in which the vessel was quite badly damaged; it was, say the accounts, 'torn apart and broken by the fury of the sea' and £5 6s.6d. had to be spent on repairs, which occupied seven men for eight days. It has been suggested that the damage was the result of bad workmanship, but this cannot be so, as the Exchequer accepted the cost of repair as well; there is ample evidence in medieval records that the Exchequer made certain that those responsible for bad workmanship had to pay to make good any faults.

☞ *See also Shipyards*

GARRETT, JACOB

A brother of Richard Garrett of Leiston, Jacob set up in business in Ipswich as a whitesmith (one who works with tinplate), coachsmith and bell-hanger. In 1802 he set up an iron foundry in premises earlier

One of the mile markers made by Jacob Garrett at his foundry on St Margaret's Green for the Little Yarmouth Turnpike Trust.

occupied by John Cobbold, on the corner of St Margaret's Green and Cobbold Street, and in 1803 he was advertising for 'old cast iron' needed urgently 'to execute an unusual order for Government'. Among his productions were the cast-iron mile markers for the Little Yarmouth Turnpike and other main roads, such as that from Darsham to Bungay, which bear dates about 1818; in spite of accidents and road improvements, many of these survive, including one outside the Mulberry Tree public house, now renamed the Milestone. When St Nicholas Church at Harwich was rebuilt in 1821, Garrett cast the columns of the nave arcade and the window tracery. In 1817 he branched out into supplying blacksmiths and others with bar iron from a warehouse opposite his foundry, and this trade was carried on by his family after his death. His grave is in Farnham churchyard, with others of his family.

GARRICK, DAVID

That most famous of actors, David Garrick, made his first appearance on the stage in 1741 at the Playhouse next to the Tankard Inn, formerly the house of Sir Humphrey Wingfield in Tacket Street. Having come to the town with a company of comedians brought from London by William Giffard, manager of the Goodman's Fields theatre there, Davy Garrick took the part of the African slave Aboan in Thomas Southerne's tragedy *Oroonoko*.

The fledgling actor seems to have been rather lacking in confidence at that early stage in his brilliant career. His biographer, Thomas Davies, reveals that 'under the disguise of a black countenance, he hoped to escape being known, should it be his misfortune not to please'. His confidence was soon boosted by his reception, for 'in every essay he gave such delight to the audience, that they gratified him with constant and loud proofs of their approbation'.
☛ *See also Lyceum*

GILES, CARL

The best-known and best-loved of British newspaper cartoonists was Carl Giles of the *Daily Express*, who worked from a studio in Princes Street, Ipswich. He is commemorated by a statue by Ipswich-born sculptor Miles Robinson of the redoubtable Grandma and the twins on the extended pavement at the junction of Princes Street and Queen Street; the bronze was sponsored by Express Group Newspapers and unveiled in September 1993 by comedian Warren Mitchell in the presence of Johnny Speight and Carl Giles himself. Giles trained as a film animator in Wardour Street after leaving school at 14 and later worked on the first Technicolor cartoon made in Britain for Alexander Korda. When his contract came to an end he was invited to join the Disney team in Hollywood, but for domestic reasons he declined and instead came to Ipswich to join Roland Davies, who had set up

Miles Robinson's statue of the Giles family, erected as a memorial to the cartoonist. Unnoticed by Grandma, the twins feed sausages to the dog.

an animation studio in Museum Street. Giles had a key role in a series of cartoon films featuring Steve the Horse, a character created by Roland Davies that appeared regularly in a strip cartoon entitled 'Come on Steve' in the *Sunday Express*; he trained the animator and tracers who worked on the six Steve films. These were all black-and-white films; a seventh Steve cartoon was to have been filmed in colour, but it never got beyond the planning stage before the studio folded up. His later cartoons in the *Daily Express* and *Sunday Express*, appearing throughout the Second World War and for many years after it, made him famous; the annual compilations published in limp covers by Express Group Newspapers are now collectors' items, and early issues fetch high prices. He also produced book jackets for Bob Arbib's *Here We Are Together* and *A Suffolk Garland for The Queen*; the latter was published for the queen's visit to Suffolk in 1961.

See David Cleveland, *East Anglia on Film* (Poppyland Publishing, 1987)

GIPPING, RIVER

Today the river that flows past Stowmarket and has its source in or near the village of Gipping is universally known as the River Gipping (pronounced with hard 'G'); its tributary that flows from Rattlesden to join it on the outskirts of Stowmarket is known as the River Rat or the Rattlesden River. At Horseshoe Weir or just below, the Gipping changes its name to Orwell, by which name it is known to its confluence with the Stour in Harwich harbour.

There is some evidence that until the eighteenth century the whole river from Rattlesden to the sea was known as the Orwell, and the stream flowing into Stowmarket from the northward was considered a tributary; there is an Orwell Meadow in Rattlesden. Early maps including Saxton (1575) and Speed (1610) clearly mark the river from Rattlesden towards Ipswich as the Orwell, but it has to be admitted that the accuracy of these maps is open to question.

Much later maps of Ipswich show the river splitting into two channels above Handford Bridge and rejoining near Stoke Bridge. The one that flows along the edge of the valley towards Handford Mill is usually marked as the Gipping, while the main channel flowing down the middle of the valley is often delineated 'The salt water'. The more northerly channel is clearly artificial, but it is of great antiquity: it already existed in AD 970. Archaeologists have found a Roman settlement beside it, and the channel may have been excavated during the Roman occupation of Britain.

☛ *See also Orwell, River; Stowmarket Navigation*

GLYDE, JOHN

Best known today for his books *The Moral, Social and Religious Condition of Ipswich* and *Illustrations of Old Ipswich*, Glyde was born in a house in Eagle

Street in 1823. A hairdresser's son, he began work in his father's shop at the age of 15 but later went to London, returning to Ipswich in 1844 and setting up his own business as a hairdresser, though he later gave this up in favour of bookselling. In 1841 he won a five-guinea (£5.25) prize offered by the Mechanics' Institute (now the Ipswich Institute) for an essay on 'Ipswich considered in its social and commercial position'. In enlarged form this was published as *The Moral, Social and Religious Condition of Ipswich in the Nineteenth Century* in 1850. His other books included *The New Suffolk Garland*, and he took a leading part in promoting social reform, though a district nursing association which he established in 1866 failed. He is said to have led a quiet, simple life, and his white hair and silver beard led one small child to say that he was 'like old Father Christmas'. He died in 1905.

GOLDING, WILLIAM

The first and only master of Wolsey's College at Ipswich, William Golding was invited by Cardinal Wolsey from Eton to serve as master under William Capon, dean of the college. When Wolsey fell from power, Golding ensured continuity in the education of his boys by staying on as master of the refounded grammar school until 1539, when he returned to a fellowship at Eton.
☛ *See also Wolsey, Thomas*

GORDON, DR WILLIAM

The Reverend William Gordon became assistant minister of Tacket Street Congregational Church in 1754, and on the death of the minister, the Reverend William Notcutt, was appointed to succeed him. He remained in charge of the Tacket Street church until 1764, when he left Ipswich to take up another post. He later went to America, where he supported the colonists during the War of Independence and, it is said, became private secretary to George Washington. Returning to England after American independence, he served as minister of St Neots Congregational Church in Huntingdonshire from 1789 to 1802, when he and his wife moved back to Ipswich and to Tacket Street church. Dr Gordon assisted the minister for a time, but died in 1807 and was buried in the graveyard of the Tacket Street church. Mrs Gordon died in 1816.
☛ *See also Barnard, John*

GRAFTON WAY

Constructed as part of a new road system in the 1990s, Grafton Way is named after the Type 23 frigate HMS *Grafton*, a warship which has been adopted by the town. In 2004 the vessel was patrolling the Arabian Gulf in the aftermath of the war with Iraq.

GRAMMAR SCHOOL

Education was important in Ipswich, where a child over 14 was deemed to have come of age and to be able to buy or sell property if he or she could count and measure; in 1344, a boy of 19 proved in court that he could count out 20s. and measure twelve ells of cloth 'well and sufficiently' and was judged to be capable of engaging in trade. Just how early there was a school at Ipswich is uncertain, but there exists a school bill for 1416–17 for Alexander de la Pole, from Wingfield; it includes 5s. 'to Master William Bury, for teaching the said Alexander for 3 terms of the year' and 6s. 8d. to 'the wife of the said Master William, for her good work done concerning the said Alexander'. William Bury presumably ran the school in his house in the parish of St Nicholas, but in 1483 Richard Felaw left his house opposite the Blackfriars church in Foundation Street, then known as St Edmund Pountney Lane, as a permanent home for the Grammar School. When Thomas Wolsey set up his college, it absorbed the Grammar School, which seemed likely to be lost when Wolsey fell from power and Henry VIII seized the buildings.

Thomas Cromwell is given the credit for ensuring that the Grammar School survived, by persuading the king to re-endow the school. William Golding, who had been master of the cardinal's college, stayed on as master and in 1537 with another man took a lease of what seems to have been the refectory of the Blackfriars; in 1614 the refectory became the schoolroom. The school remained in the former Blackfriars until 1852, when it moved to new premises in Henley Road; the foundation stone had been laid by Prince Albert on 4 July 1851 after he had attended the annual meeting of the British Association for the Advancement of Science in Ipswich. Those Elizabethan-style buildings, designed by Christopher Fleury, are still home to what is now known as Ipswich School, though many other buildings have been added since.

See John Blatchly, *A Famous Antient Seed-Plot of Learning* (Ipswich School, 2003)

☛ *See also Argentine, Richard; Felaw, Richard; Felaw's House; Golding, William; Wolsey, Thomas*

GREAT COLMAN STREET

This new street was cut through from Northgate opposite the Assembly Rooms to Major's Corner in the 1830s. It seems likely to have been named after the Colman family, who owned property in the area in the late eighteenth century. There was also a Little Colman Street connecting Great Colman Street with Carr Street at the side of the *East Anglian Daily Times* offices; it disappeared when the Carr Street precinct, later renamed Eastgates, was developed.

GREENWAYS PROJECT

Set up in 1994 by Suffolk County Council, Ipswich Borough Council and the Babergh and Suffolk Coastal district councils, and with grant aid from what was then the Countryside Commission, the Greenways countryside project is aimed at providing opportunities for local people to enjoy high-quality countryside in the area surrounding the town. The area covered by the project is largely contained by the A14 and A12 roads, though it extends east of the A12 at Martlesham to link up with the Suffolk Coast and Heaths Project. About a quarter of the population of Suffolk lives and works in the project area, which includes the Orwell Estuary Special Protection Area, the Suffolk Coast and Heaths Area of Outstanding Natural Beauty, six Sites of Special Scientific Interest, forty-six County Wildlife Sites, the Suffolk River Valleys Environmentally Sensitive Area, two Special Landscape Areas, six Local Nature Reserves and a large number of Local Wildlife Sites. A current source of conflict is the plan for a road from the A14 just to the north of the Orwell Bridge to link with the dock complex on the Orwell, which if built would run through the Orwell Country Park and do great damage to a number of wildlife sites.
☛ *See also Belstead Brook*

GREENWICH

Grenewic is listed in Domesday Book as being in Carlford Hundred, so at that time it lay outside the bounds of the town. Later, the borough bounds were extended to include what became known as Greenwich Farm. The farm buildings stood a quarter-mile south of Cliff Brewery. It is clear that the name is a very old one, and in spite of what has sometimes been surmised it has no link whatever with Greenwich Hospital, the charity operating the Royal Hospital School at Holbrook.

GREY COAT SCHOOL

Earliest of the charity schools promoted by members of the Established Church, the Grey Coat School for boys in Curriers Lane was opened in 1709 by 'several worthy gentlemen and clergymen … who considering that nothing in all human probability can contribute more to revive the practise of Christianity amongst us, than a careful instruction of youth in the grounds of their faith and duty … very generously contributed large sums towards the erecting and maintaining the schools'. In fact the school's success depended less on the gentlemen and tradesmen than on the devoted service of James Franks, who was master for forty-three years. For part of that time his wife Elizabeth ran the associated Blue Coat School for girls. About 1840, a former Grey Coat pupil who had become a master mariner bequeathed the charity £500, the interest on which was to pay for teaching navigation to boys who were intent on following their benefactor to sea. James Franks became teacher of navigation as well as of everything else, with the promise that when funds permitted he should have £3 for every boy taught navigation. Needless to say, they never did permit. James Franks resigned from his position in January 1874 'from failing health and strength' and died just six weeks later. Like most other charity schools, the Blue Coat and Grey Coat schools found their role taken over by the board and later the council schools, but a reminder of their existence is to be found on a building in Curriers Lane that is still in use for educational purposes.

GREYFRIARS SHOPPING CENTRE
Halfway between the Cornhill and the railway station, the Greyfriars complex was built when the government was planning to more than double the population of Ipswich in order to relieve pressure on London. When the government decided against the plan and decreed that Ipswich should grow only naturally, the dull concrete shopping centre and office complex was left stranded on the far side of a major new road which, in spite of the complicated Greyfriars underpass, cut it off from the existing town centre. The provision market, ousted from the Corn Exchange, was banished to the bowels of the new development, but all attempts to breathe life into the grey monstrosity failed; shoppers were deterred first by the gloomy underpass and then by the cold stare of the towering buildings. The supermarket closed, the bank gave up the fight and Greyfriars languished dirtily until Willis, Faber & Dumas needed to expand from their award-winning glass offices on the other side of Franciscan Way and took over parts of the complex, which they greatly improved.

GRIMWADE, J.H., & SONS LTD
A very well-known outfitters with a shop on the corner of the Cornhill and Westgate Street, Grimwade's closed in 1996 when the directors decided that, with no heirs to take on the business, they did not wish to see it continue as other than a family firm. The business was started in 1844 by Richard Grimwade, a tailor and woollen draper, in Westgate Street. Twenty years later, Richard's business seemed about to fail. He left Ipswich, but the business was carried on by his sixteen-year-old son John Henry Grimwade, who had to shoulder the responsibility of maintaining his mother and his six brothers and sisters. John Henry succeeded where his father had not, and by the time he retired at the age of seventy the shop had been extended along Westgate Street and also on to the Cornhill. Elected to the town council at his fourth attempt in 1887, John Henry was mayor in 1904–5 and remained on the council until his death in 1929 at the age of eighty. His son Sidney Charles Grimwade was elected to the council in 1924 and was twice mayor, and his grandson Edward Charles Grimwade was mayor in 1964–5; his great-grandson Peter, who joined

the firm in 1954, was elected to the council in 1963. Although the shop closed in 1996 and has since been occupied by other businesses, Ipswich people still think of it as Grimwade's; and it is odd to find that in the 2004/05 BT Phone Book the firm was still listed, eight years after it went out of existence.

GRIMWADE STREET
Laid out in the early twentieth century to form a link between St Helen's Street and Rope Walk, this roadway took the name of Alderman Edward Grimwade. The name originally applied only to the section between these two streets. It was linked to Fore Street by Borough Road and St Clement's Church Street, and from the mid-twentieth century the name Grimwade Street was applied to these as well.

HALTEBY, JOHN DE
A fourteenth-century local politician, John de Halteby was one of the group who took power after the fall of Thomas le Rent, Thomas Stacy and others who had built up a local power-base of their own in the early 1300s. Halteby seems to have made himself generally unpopular through his political activities, and his murder in 1344 was greeted with general approval by the local inhabitants. He may have been the same John Haltebe who was miller of Horsewade Mill when it burnt down in 1336.
☛ *See also Horswade Mill*

HANDFORD MILL
This mill, referred to in documents from the thirteenth century as the mill of Hagenford, was just outside the town, beside the road to Handford Bridge. It may originally have been driven by a stream running down from the Anglesea Road area, but an artificial channel was dug to bring water from a new weir built on the Gipping some way above Handford Bridge; this channel was certainly in use when the bounds of Stoke were set down in AD 970, and it is possible that it was made by the Romans, perhaps to bring water to a mill on the site of Handford Mill or nearby.

In the nineteenth century Handford Mill was an oil mill, using the power of the waterwheel to grind and crush oilseed for the extraction of oil.

HARMONY SQUARE
A nineteenth-century development of some twenty small houses north of Woodbridge Road, approached by a narrow passage. With the building of Lacey Street later in the century Harmony Square was squeezed between that new street and Woodbridge Road and at such an angle that it seemed to relate to neither. Bombed in the Second World War, it was cleared in the 1950s.

HIPPODROME

Designed by Frank Matcham, a leading theatre designer of the early twentieth century and architect of the London Coliseum, the Hippodrome in St Nicholas Street was built in 1905 by E.H. Bostock (of Bostock & Wombwell's Menagerie), to be run in tandem with another Hippodrome in Norwich: 'it is a great advantage to offer artistes two or more weeks' engagements in the same neighbourhood,' he said. Matcham made a name for his ability to fit theatres into the most difficult of sites, and the Hippodrome had to be squeezed between St Nicholas Street, Cutler Street and St Nicholas Church Lane. The plaster decorations of the auditorium were lavish, the ornamentation of the exterior striking if restrained. Teams of elephants as well as human stars performed at the Hippodrome, but after a quarter of a century as a theatre it became a cinema, reverting to revue in 1941; many well-known stars appeared there during and after the Second World War. In 1957 it became a ballroom, and then a bingo hall, and was demolished in 1985 to make way for offices.

HISTORIC CHURCHES TRUST, IPSWICH

In medieval times Ipswich had a wealth of fine churches, each serving a parish and in use not only on Sundays but daily, as the focus of parochial life. Today, with the population having moved away from the town centre into the newer residential areas, some of these churches are no longer in use, and the Ipswich Historic Churches Trust is entrusted with caring for them. The trust was formed in 1979 and took over the churches of St Nicholas, St Peter, St Clement, St Stephen and St Lawrence on long lease from Ipswich Borough Council; St Stephen's has become the town's Tourist Information Office and St Nicholas's has been handed back to the Diocese of St Edmundsbury to become a diocesan resource and conference centre. With help from the borough council and from English Heritage, the trust has carried out repairs to the churches in its care, with the long-term aim of finding alternative uses for them.

HOLY WELLS

There were several sacred wells in the area, one of them being the *Haligwille* or holy well that was a landmark on the bounds of Stoke, set down in Old English in 970; it seems to have been a spring on the hillside on Fir Tree Farm. The Ipswich torcs – gold ceremonial collars from the first century BC, supposed to have been worn by chieftains of the Iron Age tribes inhabiting the Ipswich area – were discovered in 1968 on a slope of the hill 'overlooking a tributary of the Belstead Brook' at map reference TM13684273; it is thought by some archaeologists that this tributary could be the stream flowing down from the holy well, and that the torcs might have been deposited beside the holy well as some kind of offering. The springs in Holywells Park seem not to have been sacred wells; the name is said in this case to be derived from 'hollow well'.

☛ *See also Torcs, the Ipswich; Holywells Park*

HOLYWELLS PARK

On rising ground overlooking both town and river and containing natural springs that gave it the name of Holywells, this park is reputed to have been the site of the manor held before the Norman Conquest by Queen Edith, wife of Edward the Confessor. In the park is a large moated site, which is probably where the Bishop of Norwich stayed whenever his duties brought him into Suffolk. Holywells mansion was built in the park about 1814 by John Cobbold, who made it the family home; the park and mansion were presented to the town in the 1920s by Lord Woodbridge, but after the Second World War the mansion became derelict, and it was demolished in 1962, leaving only some outbuildings on the site. Cobbold used the water of the Holywells in his Cliff Brewery, and also supplied it to about 600 houses in the eastern part of the town.

☛ *See also Cliff Brewery; Cobbold, John; Wykes Bishop*

Holywells Mansion seen across one of the ponds fed by the Holywells, in a nineteenth-century photograph by William Vick.

HORSE TRAMS
☛ *See Trams, Horse*

HORSEWADE, THE
A ford over the northern arm of the Gipping leading to the Corporation Marshes. The river was presumably too deep to be forded by people on foot, but sufficiently shallow for a horse to wade across. The name appears in the Anglo-Saxon bounds of Stoke, set down in 970. After the founding in the thirteenth century of the Greyfriars this crossing became known as Friars Bridge, though it is likely that it remained a ford and that an actual structure over the stream was not built until much later. It is apparent that, in this part of Suffolk at least, the word 'bridge' at one time implied no more than a crossing-place or ford, as with Downham Bridge.
☛ *See also Horswade Mill*

HORSWADE MILL
This watermill stood on the same stream that was used to power Handford Mill, on the site later known as Friars Bridge, between the modern Portman Road and Princes Street. It was burnt down in 1336, after which the miller, John Haltebe, expressed his willingness to rebuild the mill and was granted an eight-year lease on the strength of his undertaking. The mill disappeared some time in the mid-seventeenth century.
☛ *See also Halteby, John de*

HOSPITAL, IPSWICH AND EAST SUFFOLK
Opened in 1836, the Anglesea Road hospital cost £2,500, provided by public subscription. The original building was of two storeys, with a flight of steps leading up to the front door between four lofty columns; 'if pleasantness of

The hospital as it was built in 1836, with only two floors above ground level; a third was added in 1869.

situation, and the attainment of a pure and healthy atmosphere, enter especially into the *vade mecum* for the restoration of health, no building in the kingdom … possesses advantages exceeding this', as an 1842 guidebook put it. A third storey was added in 1869, and further buildings were added over the years until the hospital covered a considerable area. It is now the Anglesea Heights Nursing Home, its original purpose now being served by The Ipswich Hospital in Heath Road, on the site of the former Borough General Hospital.

INSTITUTE, THE IPSWICH

A survivor from an age when for many people education was no more than a dream and knowledge of the world beyond their own town was fragmentary, the Ipswich Institute has changed to suit an entirely different world. Yet in essence it still performs the service it was founded to provide. It had its beginning in a circular, put out during the winter of 1823–4 by John Raw, whose bookshop and circulating library was in the Buttermarket, suggesting the formation of an organisation to provide lectures for working men on the lines of those established by Dr George Birkbeck in Glasgow and London.

Nearly a year went by before a meeting was presided over by William Batley and it was agreed to establish a Mechanics' Institution. Its objects were 'the instruction of the members in the principles of the arts they practice … and in the various branches of science and useful knowledge'. The first president was John FitzGerald, the father of Edward FitzGerald, the linguist and translator of *The Rubáiyát of Omar Khayyám*, and among the supporters was Robert Ransome, the ironfounder.

Among the main activities in the early years of the Mechanics' Institute were lectures on scientific subjects given by local men who were

A subscriber's ticket acknowledging receipt of nine shillings (45p) subscription to the Ipswich Institute, formerly the Mechanics' Institute, for the quarter July to October 1898. Such an amount would probably have ruled out most 'mechanics'.

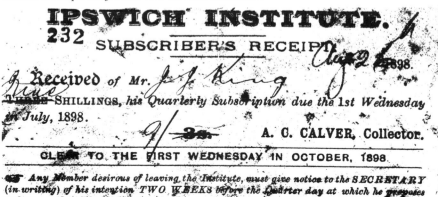

knowledgeable about such matters. There was even a lady lecturer on one occasion, but she attracted few listeners; it was considered too daring an innovation for the time.

In 1834 the Institute moved to a shop in Tavern Street previously occupied by Samuel Belcher Chapman, 'chymist & druggist', which was acquired by a company of shareholders with 200 shares of £5 each; in 1877 the Institute purchased the remaining shares. As time went by, further moves were proposed, but instead adjoining premises in Tower Street were bought and a lecture hall built there. The educational nature of the Institute remained, but it was found that the 'artisans' (the ordinary working people) were not attracted to the classes. When the Reverend F. Barham Zincke inaugurated the Working Men's College the classes were abandoned, but not until 1893 was 'Mechanics' dropped from the title.

A Victorian member returning in the mid-twentieth century would have had few surprises. Even a suggestion that the Institute should have a telephone was successfully resisted until 1931. The lecture hall was leased to Poole's Picture Palace from 1909 to 1940; seven years later, after being used as a club for British and Allied Servicemen during the war, it became the Ipswich Arts Theatre.

During its 180-year history the Institute has had its ups and downs, yet it is still valued by its membership of more than two thousand. It recently opened a new restaurant, it puts on an enterprising programme of talks, visits and study groups, and it gives support to local projects, including educational activities, theatres, museums and the arts. No less important, it provides its members with a pleasant haven in the hustle and bustle of twenty-first-century Ipswich.

See Eric H. Hanson, *An Historical Essay of the Ipswich Institute 1925–1987* (Ipswich Institute, 1989)

☛ *See also Ransome, Robert; Poole's Picture Palace; Working Men's College*

IPSWICH BUILDING PRESERVATION TRUST
☛ *See Building Preservation Trust*

IPSWICH BUILDING SOCIETY
☛ *See Freehold Land Society, Ipswich & Suffolk*

IPSWICH JOURNAL
One of the earliest local newspapers in Britain, the *Ipswich Journal* was established by John Bagnall 'at the Printing Office in St. Mary-Elms' in 1720. It was later published by William Craighton, printer and bookseller at the Stationers' Arms in the Buttermarket, and when he died in 1761 his

sister Elizabeth and a nephew, William Jackson, carried on producing the paper. As a result of a dispute following Jackson's bankruptcy two rival versions of the *Ipswich Journal* appeared from 1774 to 1777, Mrs Craighton publishing the *Original Ipswich Journal* and another printer producing the *Ipswich Journal*.

For one week in 1867 when the Royal Show was held at Bury St Edmunds, the *Journal* came out every day, giving it a claim to be the first daily paper in the region, special staff being brought in from London to produce the newspaper. It was a commendable experiment that was stifled by the inability to carry it further due to lack of financial resources. The *Journal* ceased publication in 1902.

IPSWICH PUDDING

An almond pudding for which the recipe is to be found in such old 'receipt books' as the *Lady's Companion* of 1836. One version follows:

$1/4$ pint single cream
$1^{1}/_{2}$oz fresh white breadcrumbs
2oz castor sugar
4oz ground almonds
4 drops almond essence
3 eggs
A little butter
Split almonds for decoration

Grease 2pt oven dish. Warm cream and pour over breadcrumbs, stir in sugar, ground almonds and almond essence. Beat one egg and two yolks and add to mixture. Whisk remaining egg whites till stiff and fold into almond mixture. Pour into dish, add dots of butter and split almonds. Bake in slow oven [325° F or gas mark 2] for about $1^{1}/_{2}$ hours or until pudding is well risen and golden brown. Serve at once. Serves 4–6 people.

IPSWICH WARE

A form of Anglo-Saxon pottery made on a large scale in the Ipswich kilns from the mid-seventh century onwards, the earliest post-Roman wheel-thrown pottery made in Britain. Examples of this pottery have been found throughout East Anglia, and in coastal areas of Essex and Kent, and also at places along the rivers Nene and Welland; the distribution of find sites suggests that the pottery was carried by sea and river from the Orwell to the places where it was used.

ISAAC LORD'S

A remarkable survival of a Tudor merchant's house and business premises, between Fore Street and the quayside, the Isaac Lord complex deserves to be one of the tourist sights of Ipswich. Isaac Lord bought the property from the Cobbold family in 1900, but the man for whom it was built is so far unknown. The earliest part of the range facing Fore Street dates from the early 1400s; this building was truncated when a new house with a jettied gable facing the street was erected in 1636, as recorded on the carved bressumer, the beam supporting the overhanging upper storey. The house was occupied by the Lord family until about the 1980s. Behind it is a warehouse, known as the Saleroom because that is thought to be the part where customers came to inspect the merchant's cloth for sale, when Ipswich was exporting woollen cloth to the Continent. Both the house and the Saleroom, which has a crownpost roof, are listed Grade 1 as buildings of historic and architectural interest. Across the bottom of the yard, which is approached by a waggon entry from the street, is a crosswing, which was built between 1530 and 1550, again with a waggon entry under one end. The heavy windbraces of the oak roof as well as the herringbone brick infilling between the timber frame mark this as a building of high status, albeit an industrial building. The waggon entry led to a private quay where ships loaded bales of Suffolk woollen cloth destined for ports in the Low Countries and possibly more distant places. More recently, the buildings between the crosswing and the quay were used as maltings, producing malt from Suffolk barley for the Cliff Brewery and possibly for breweries on the Thames, which absorbed vast amounts of Ipswich malt. The kiln in which the malt was dried was in 1984 converted into a public house.

Stuart Cooper, the son of Reginald Cooper who joined Isaac Lord in 1930 and helped develop the corn and coal trade of the firm, has spent 25 years restoring the buildings and finding new uses for them. The west side of the site has been fully restored, and provides a home for the John Russell Art Gallery in Wherry Lane and a number of offices.

JEWS' CEMETERY

Set up in the eighteenth century by the local Hebrew community, the Jews' cemetery was at the end of Salthouse Lane, off Salthouse Street. Like some other old byways, Salthouse Lane has been closed and taken into neighbouring property, but the cemetery is still surrounded by its brick wall at the back of what were the offices of R. & W. Paul. It contains thirty-six gravestones with Hebrew inscriptions, most of them now illegible. The St Clement's parish boundary runs through the cemetery, and there are parish boundary stones above the door in the east wall and in the north wall. The little cemetery is no longer in use for burials.

JOHN'S NESS

About two miles below the Common Quay on the east bank of the Orwell is John's Ness, where John Barnard built the *Hampshire* in 1740. The water was deeper there than in the town, but also vessels could be launched into the length of Backagain Reach, which ran across the river from one shore to the other. The name possibly derived from King John's Ness, though why the king who granted the town its charter should have been thus commemorated is unknown.

☞ *See also Barnard, John; Orwell, River; Shipyards*

KEY STREET

In spite of the key-shaped weather vane topping the tower of St Mary-at-Quay Church, the name of the street derives quite simply from the earlier spelling of quay.

KING STREET

The name is now applied only to the street running from Princes Street and Queen Street to Elm Street and Arcade Street, but it was once also used for the road at the side of the Corn Exchange and Town Hall, from Princes Street/Queen Street to the Cornhill. There is evidence that the whole highway from Stoke Bridge to Cornhill was at one time known as Kingstreet; it is shown by this name on Ogilby's map in the seventeenth century, and the division into St Peter's Street, St Nicholas Street and Queen Street appears to be later. It has

The Sickle Inn and the King's Head Commercial Inn stood in that part of King Street that ran beside the Town Hall, now a part of Princes Street. They came down in 1878–79 to make way for the new Corn Exchange.

been suggested that the name may date from Saxon times, when the Wuffinga kings of East Anglia might have had a royal residence on Cornhill.

KING'S HOSPITAL

The former house of Lord Curson in Silent Street, used as the Suffolk residence of the Bishops of Norwich in the seventeenth century, became a hospital for sick and wounded seamen of the Navy during the First Dutch War of 1652–4. Some of the seamen wounded in a battle in 1653 off the Gabbard, some 50 miles from Harwich, were brought upriver to Ipswich in the *Tenth Whelp* and the bailiffs, Richard Puplett and Nicholas Phillips, received a letter from a Navy Commissioner asking them to provide for other sick men from warships ordered into Harwich. The bailiffs dutifully appointed surgeons to care for the men and spent £80 a week looking after the sick and wounded, of whom there were at least eighty in the town; they found it extremely difficult to obtain repayment of all the money that was spent. Later Nicholas Phillips wrote that there were 'neere a thousand sick and wounded soldiers and seamen in the towne' and complained of the town's 'inability of relieving them, wee have expended all the moneys we could command ... We are likelie to see these poore people perish for want of support.' In the burials register of St Nicholas Church there is an entry for 'Burialls Anno 1666 of Seamen out of the kings hospitall at Cussom house that weer buryed in the p'ish of St Nicolas in Ipswich'.

☛ *See also Curson's House*

LYCEUM

The old theatre at which David Garrick had made his debut, 'a small and unimportant building in Tacket Street', was acquired by the Salvation Army

The Lyceum Theatre in Carr Street in the 1920s, with one of the electric trams in the distance, followed by a lady on a bicycle.

as its citadel in 1892. The gap left by its closure had been filled by the Lyceum Theatre in Carr Street, designed by London architect Walter Emden and built 'in the Italian style' in 1890–91 at a cost of £9,000. Its 1,300-seater auditorium was a confection of yellow and gold, liberally sprinkled with Shakespearian mottoes. In the 1920s it was acquired by E.H. Bostock and became a cinema. It closed in 1936 and was demolished to make way for a branch of Great Universal Stores of Manchester.

MALTING

With Suffolk farms producing some of the best malting barley in Britain, it is not surprising that malt has been processed in Ipswich for hundreds of years. References in the corporation archives indicate that malting was one of the most important trades in the town in the Middle Ages, when steps were taken to ensure that only burgesses (the freemen of the borough) should participate. In the eighteenth and nineteenth centuries, some old merchants' houses were turned into maltings to satisfy demand from brewers locally and in London for good malt.

Malt is partially-germinated grain, normally barley. During germination, the starch in the grain is broken down to produce maltose, which is turned into sugar in the brewer's mash tun; the sugar is then fermented to produce alcohol during brewing. The barley is first steeped in water and then spread on the malting floor to germinate, being turned daily to aerate it and to prevent the rootlets matting together as they grow. At just the right moment

This attractive malting in Princes Street was built in 1866 and continued to turn out good malt for nearly a century. It is now serving as an unusual nightclub.

it is loaded into the kiln (or kell, as it is known in Suffolk) to be dried over a smokeless fire, thus bringing germination to an end.

Until the end of the nineteenth century, malt was produced in traditional floor maltings, but during the twentieth century various methods of pneumatic malting were introduced. In this, instead of being spread thinly on the malting floor, the grain is germinated in a tank or 'street' and air is pumped through the germinating grain, which is periodically turned by large mechanical turners. In 1963 R. & W. Paul (Maltsters) Ltd installed a German-designed *Wanderhaufen* or 'moving batch' plant at their Albion Malting, which was the first of its kind to be constructed in Britain. Regular cargoes of malt from this dockside malting were in 2004 still being despatched by sea to Beck's brewery in Bremen, as well as to British breweries, but the malting has now closed.
☛ *See also Paul, R. & W.*

MANGANESE BRONZE LTD

One of the earliest companies to move part of its production from the London area, the Manganese Bronze & Brass Co Ltd (as it then was) established a works on the Hadleigh Road Industrial Estate in 1916. Five years later the rolling mill and forge were moved from London to Ipswich. Plans were made in 1937 for a large new extrusion plant, completed in 1940, in time to play a very important part in making special alloys for war purposes. The company had already in 1932 installed a plant to make self-lubricating bearings from powder metals, a development that was to have a considerable impact on the motor industry and on engineering generally. After the Second World War the company moved to a new factory on the Elton Park Estate, not far from the original works, which was in due course given up. The sintering process, in which powder metal is coalesced to form a body of the required shape under heat and pressure, originally used for the production of maintenance-free self-lubricating bearings, is now employed to make a much wider range of products.

MARKET CROSS

The ornate structure, surmounted by a lead figure of Justice, that was the Market Cross stood in the middle of the Cornhill for nearly 200 years until it was demolished in 1812, to the considerable regret of some if not all of the townspeople. The figure of Justice, given in 1723 by Francis Negus, then one of the town's MPs, took on a new personality as Ceres with her horn of plenty and was moved to the front of the Corn Exchange built by George Gooding.

The first Market Cross, given by a well-to-do merchant, Edmund Daundy, was erected in 1510, perhaps as a preaching cross. Daundy, who was bailiff in the year he gave the cross, was a relative of Cardinal Wolsey. Its

An old print of the Market Cross, with the former St Mildred's Church turned into the Town Hall in the background. Both disappeared in the nineteenth century, though not without regret in the case of the Cross.

replacement was a more flamboyant affair, an octagonal structure with an ogee-shaped lead-covered roof and a lofty central post erected about 1628. We do not know how much the building of the new cross cost, but we do know that Benjamin Osborne had in 1610 left £50 towards it. For some reason the corporation seems to have taken almost twenty years to persuade his executors to hand the money over, and then they came up with only £44.

In 1660 the corporation gave orders that the Cross should be 'beautified' in celebration of the Restoration of King Charles II, and from time to time money was spent from town funds on repairs. When in 1812 it was decided to demolish the Cross 'in furtherance of the improvements that were then taking place' G.R. Clarke tells us that it was only pulled down 'with considerable difficulty, as the timber, and every part of it, were in excellent preservation'. The historian lamented that, 'As a relic of antiquity, we cannot but regret its loss.'

☞ **See also Cornhill**

MARTIN & NEWBY

Founded by John Martin in 1873 and opened on 21 September that year, the shop in Fore Street known for most of the next 130 years as Martin and Newby's supplied Ipswich handymen with everything they could possibly need and built up a reputation as a place where you could find things you could not buy anywhere else. Sadly, it closed down in June 2004. John Martin not only operated what was known at the beginning as a 'birmingham and sheffield warehouse' selling ironmongery and cutlery but was also a boot and shoe manufacturer. Martin employed his nephew, Frederick Newby, who had served an apprenticeship with Saxmundham ironmongers Wells & Sons and lived next door to him in Warwick Road, as manager of the hardware shop, purchasing stock to the value of just £97. Following Martin's death in 1885 Frederick Newby was lent £100 by a friend of his father's and obtained a loan on a house he was purchasing to buy into the business, and in so doing seems to have got the Martin family out of a financial dilemma. In 1897 the firm bought the old buildings of the shoe shop, demolished them and built a new hardware shop on the site. Newby was joined in 1906 by Edward Atkinson, but the firm continued to be called Martin & Newby, though the last Martin left in 1899 because Newby refused to pay him more. Newby died in 1933, and three generations of the Atkinson family have since then been at the head of the firm, which expanded significantly in the mid-twentieth century. They set up an electrical department which, among other things, installed an electrical system, including floodlighting, at Helmingham Hall in the years after the Second World War.

MARTYRS' MEMORIAL

Nine people who suffered martyrdom in Ipswich for their Protestant beliefs are commemorated on the Martyrs' Memorial in Christchurch Park, which was erected in 1903. The first was Nicholas Peke, who was burnt at the stake in 1538, and the next was a man named Kerby, who was sentenced with Roger Clark of Mendlesham in 1546. Clark was sent to Bury St Edmunds to be burnt, while Kerby was burnt at the stake on the Cornhill in Ipswich. Others listed on the memorial are Robert Samuel (1555), who had been removed from his benefice at East Bergholt for being married, Agnes Potten, Joan Trunchfield and John Tudson (1556), and Alice Driver, Alexander Gouch and William Pikes (1558), all of whom suffered death by burning.

MODEL RAILWAY, CREWCHESTER

Hidden away in the garden of a quite normal house in a normal Ipswich street, the Crewchester Model Railway was not so much an ordinary model layout as a working railway in miniature, with a working timetable and three signal cabins with block instruments salvaged from old signal boxes and communication bells operating in the same way as on a full-size railway. Yet the 0-gauge layout set up by Jack Ray in 1961 depended on clockwork locomotives, with the speed controlled by regulators taken from telephone dialling mechanisms. The railway could be operated by four really experienced people, but the normal complement was at least double that number. The heart of the railway's workforce was a band of enthusiastic youngsters who spent a great deal of their spare time not only operating the trains but also carrying out essential maintenance and doing all the other work that was needed. One of the two termini, named Ravensmoor Queen Street, was among the most ambitious stations ever attempted on a model layout, with one of its seven platforms no less than 17ft (5.2m) long.

MOSS, COLIN
Few people have recorded life in working-class Ipswich in the way the artist Colin Moss has. Born in Ipswich in 1914, Colin lost his father in the slaughter of Passchendaele when he was three, and after the war his mother moved away from Ipswich; he grew up in Devonport. After service in the Second World War, Colin Moss obtained a post at Ipswich School of Art. He found the town of his birth a drab place: 'When I think back it always reminds me of a Coronation Street scene really,' he recalls, 'It wasn't like a town in the south at all. In those days I always felt that it was like a town from the north that had somehow slipped down a couple of hundred miles and got here!' He found the art school a very formal institution, and the only member of staff who went out of his way to make him feel welcome was Leonard Squirrel; nevertheless, he remained there for the rest of his teaching career.

See Chloe Bennett, *Colin Moss: Life Observed* (Malthouse Press, 1996)

MOUNT STREET
According to Edward White's 1849 map, Lower Mount Street ran from Black Horse Lane to Lady Lane; and Upper Mount Street ran from Lady

A painting of the Mount as it was in the nineteenth century, with Mr Punch bludgeoning his way through life before a large and enthusiastic audience.

Lane to Mill Street (the latter now the upper part of Portman Road). The Mount was where the present Police Station stands and may have been the remains of the eleventh-century castle motte or mound. In the early twentieth century this was an area of rundown working-class housing, cleared away under the mid-century slum clearance scheme. In the mid-nineteenth century there was also a Mount Street in the Potteries on the east side of the town; this later became part of Regent Street.

☛ *See also Castle*

MUSEUM, THE IPSWICH

The pilastered building once occupied by the Ipswich Museum still stands in Museum Street, close to the Arcade Street corner and opposite the Methodist Church. It was designed by an Irish-born architect, Christopher Fleury, who a little later designed the new grammar school in Henley Road. When it was opened on 15 December 1847, the museum was said to be 'more particularly for the benefit of the working classes', an objective that marked it out from most contemporary establishments of the kind. One of its promoters was the Reverend Professor J.S. Henslow, who was Charles Darwin's tutor at Cambridge and the incumbent of the Suffolk village of Hitcham; he took a

The Victorian buildings to which the Ipswich Museum moved in 1881. These premises also included an art gallery on the left, the 'Victoria Library', and the School of Art.

keen interest in what would today be known as adult education. Sadly, the regular lectures given at the museum, 'to which tickets for free admission are distributed among the working classes', failed to attract more than a minority of those at whom they were aimed, even though some were given by Henslow himself, and others by the Astronomer Royal, Sir George Biddell Airy.

Nonetheless, it is said that in the 1870s the average attendance at these lectures was over 400 people. The first curator was Dr William Barnard Clarke, well known at the time as a naturalist. In the beginning the museum was free on Wednesdays and Fridays, and for the rest of the week a small charge was levied; one cannot help wondering how many working people were able to visit on the free days, since most were at work from Monday to at least lunchtime on Saturday. After the Corporation took over management in 1853 it was thrown open free of charge for four days a week, and remained open on Wednesday and Friday evenings until 9pm.

The Museum Committee decided in 1878 to erect a new building for the Museum and also the School of Art, which had been taken over by the corporation in 1874. A site was acquired in High Street, originally intended for a new church; the building was designed by Horace Chesterton and was opened with much ceremony on 27 July 1881, at the same time as the new lock entrance to the Wet Dock and the new Post Office on Cornhill. A proposal by the borough council to close the High Street building to the public, using it merely as an exhibit store, and to retain only Christchurch Mansion as a museum open to the public was fortunately not put into effect. The proposal no doubt had its effect in scotching the town's application for city status in 2000.

MUSEUM STREET
When Pennington made his map in the 1770s, the area between Westgate Street and Elm Street was entirely taken up with gardens, but in the 1840s plans were made for a new street linking Westgate and Elm streets. An opening for the new street was made through part of what had been Seckford House in Westgate Street and the roadway was constructed as far as the museum, opened in 1847. At that point the road turned to the east, though it did not link up with Elm Street until in 1850 an archway was made through one of the houses to provide that link. When Thursby's Lane was extended in 1856 to a junction with Museum Street, the eastern leg of the latter was renamed Arcade Street and the name Museum Street was applied to the former Thursby's Lane as far as its junction with Princes Street.
☛ *See also Thursby's Lane; Westgate Street*

NELSON, LORD
Although he never stayed there, Horatio Nelson had a home in Ipswich: Roundwood on the Rushmere road. It was occupied by his wife and his

father, the Reverend Edmund Nelson, for some years. The historian G.R. Clarke tells how on 16 October 1798 there was a grand ball and supper in commemoration of Nelson's victory at the Battle of the Nile. 'About eight o'clock, Lady Nelson's arrival was announced by the ringing of bells and the loud huzzas of a vast concourse of people in the street. Her ladyship was introduced into the ball-room by Admiral Sir Richard Hughes, bart., and Admiral Reeve, who conducted her to the top of the room, attended by the Rev. Mr. Nelson, the venerable father of the admiral, followed by Captain Bourchier, leading up Miss Berry, sister to Capt. Berry, of the *Vanguard*. The room was lighted up with transparencies, and variegated lamps interspersed amongst a variety of evergreens, which had a beautiful effect. Upwards of three hundred persons of distinction and fashion were present, and the evening passed off with universal hilarity and eclat.' In 1800 Lord Nelson was chosen as High Steward of the borough, and on 8 November that year he arrived at Roundwood with Sir William and Lady Hamilton. They found it locked up, as Lady Nelson had gone to London to prepare for her husband's arrival there, and they had to go to the Great White Horse for refreshment and rest before going on to London.

☛ *See also* **White Horse, Great**

NEPTUNE INN, OLD

An interesting example of a hall-house partly of fifteenth- and partly of sixteenth-century date, the Old Neptune Inn evidently began its life as one of the principal merchants' houses in the port area of Ipswich. It must have become an inn sometime in the eighteenth century: in 1777, when the property was leased by Thomas Moore to Daniel Orford it was said to be 'lately called the Neptune Inn'. Although it was seemingly not always licensed, it was an inn or a beerhouse for much of the period up to 1937, when the licence was given up. For many years, dock

Printed in Ipswich by W.S. Cowell, this 1905 postcard shows the Old Neptune with its extraordinarily crooked chimney at a time when it was still a licensed house. It was a director of Cowell's, George Bodley Scott, who restored the house in the years after the Second World War after it had ceased to be an inn.

labourers received their pay in the bar parlour, and in the early twentieth century the Breton onion boys used to take over the main bar parlour when they arrived in Ipswich, hanging their onions around the linen-fold panelling and sleeping on the floor. The premises were acquired in 1947 in a more or less derelict state by George Bodley Scott, a director of printers W.S. Cowell; during the Second World War they had been used as a store, and before that they had been occupied by an Ipswich builder as offices and stores. Mr Scott set about restoring the old house, doing much of the work himself; he made linen-fold panelling to replace that which had been removed, put in new stairs and new floors, and also restored an old barn which was almost in a state of collapse when he acquired the Neptune.

NORTH GATE

This town gate, which gave its name to Northgate Street, spanned the northern end of that street where the public house formerly known as the Halberd now stands; it is said that parts of the old gateway can still be seen in the cellars of what is now called Maginty's. Also known as the Barr Gate, this gate was demolished in 1794; the *Ipswich Journal* of 2 August that year reported that 'Monday the workmen began pulling down the building called St Margaret's Gates. This alteration will not be the least of the numerous improvements in consequence of the paving act.'
☛ *See also Bull Gate; East Gate; Walls, Town; West Gate*

OGILBY, JOHN

Responsible for the first detailed large-scale map of the town, surveyed in 1674, John Ogilby was also the man who had the job of arranging the coronation procession for Charles II. His map was engraved and printed by Thomas Steward in 1698, twenty-two years after Ogilby's death, and is surrounded by depictions of the town's parish churches and main buildings. In all that he did, Ogilby overcame every setback and succeeded, as John Aubrey says in his *Brief Lives*: 'He had such an excellent inventive and prudential wit, and master of so good address, that when he was undone he could not only shift handsomely (which is a great mastery) but he would make such rational proposals that would be embraced by rich and great men, that in a short time he could gain a good estate again; and never failed in anything he ever undertook, but always went through with profits and honour.'
☛ *See also Pennington, Joseph*

OLD BELL INN
☛ *See Bell, The Old*

Once a well-known feature of the town scene, Green & Hatfield's 'Old Curiosity Shop' between St Margaret's Street and Old Foundry Road.

OLD FOUNDRY ROAD

Running from Northgate Street to Carr Street, this highway was until the mid-nineteenth century known as St Margaret's Ditches, since the roadway ran along the line of the ditch inside the town ramparts. Robert Ransome acquired premises in St Margaret's Ditches for his foundry, which operated here until the move to the Orwell Works, completed in 1849. This Old Foundry gave a new name to the thoroughfare. Until the 1930s there were still houses here built on top of the rampart and approached by steps from the road.

☞ *See also Ransome, Robert; Orwell Works*

OLD NEPTUNE INN

☞ *See Neptune Inn, Old*

ORWELL BRIDGE

The bridge over the Orwell between Wherstead and Nacton, which incorporates the longest prestressed concrete span in Europe, was built as part of the Ipswich southern by-pass and was opened in 1982. The day before the official opening the bridge was thrown open to walkers who, led by the Mayor, Mrs Beryl James, streamed across in their hundreds; one man crossed in a wheelchair, and another led a cow over the bridge. The span over the navigation channel has a clearance of 126ft (38.3m) at high water, allowing large vessels to reach the port of Ipswich.

ORWELL, RIVER
In historic times 'the port of Orwell' referred to an anchorage in the lower part of the river, just above Harwich harbour, where the English fleet was sometimes mustered in time of war and from which laden merchantmen would take their departure for Flanders, Gascony and other destinations. The Corporation of Ipswich claimed jurisdiction over the whole estuary, from Ipswich to Harwich, and out to the Poll Head off Felixstowe. More recently, that estuary – what earlier maps called 'the salt water' – has become 'the River Orwell'. Opinion varies as to where the Gipping becomes the Orwell. Some say it is at the weir at the bottom of Constantine Road, but this was built only about 1903 to provide cooling water for the electricity generating station. A more feasible spot is Horseshoe Weir, presumably named from its original shape, below which was 'the salt water'; the artificial northern section of river known as 'the sweet water' or fresh water, now cut off by Handford Sluice, was the Gipping. The Orwell has played its part in naval history from early times: in 1338–9 Edward III assembled his fleet in the Orwell to attack France, and in 1939–45 there was much naval activity at Felixstowe, Woolverstone and Ipswich.

ORWELL WORKS
From the time they gave up the Old Foundry in 1849 until the move to Nacton Works about 1950 Ransomes occupied the Orwell Works, which spread out alongside the Wet Dock and filled much of the space between the dock and Duke Street as well as an area on the other side of Duke Street.

In 1837 William Worby, later works manager, received a summons that rather startled him, as he recalled later:

> One morning in March 1837, I was summoned to the presence of Messrs Robert and James Ransome in Mr Robert Ransome's room, which was then an upper room in the offices in St Margaret's Ditches. Mr Robert Ransome told me that they had sent for me to find a place for myself. I asked if they wanted me to leave them, whereupon Mr Robert Ransome said, 'By no means – we mean that you should go and hire malt offices or some such place, where you can take some of the men and some of the work, forming a sort of branch works, as we are getting too thick here, and we do not want you and Mr May together.'

It seems that Worby and the new partner, Charles May, had been on less than friendly terms and this was causing friction. The Ransomes, finding the business expanding, had decided that a move to new premises could solve two problems at once.

The riverside premises that Worby obtained can be seen on a panorama drawn by Edward Caley as part of the preparations for the Wet Dock scheme. There it is, between St Clement's Shipyard and an inlet off the river, with 'Orwell Iron Works' painted in white on an end wall. That was just a start; between 1837 and 1849 the new works extended along the waterfront to the south of the temporary premises, the first of the new buildings being occupied in 1841.

Completion of the firm's move to the new Orwell Works in 1849 was commemorated by a great dinner given by the partners to some 1,500 guests, including many of their valued customers in the farming industry. The workers were included, sitting at tables in the gallery and looking down on the partners and their guests on the ground floor, and prodigious quantities of beef and beer are said to have been consumed by the assembled company.
☛ *See also Ransome, Robert; Ransomes, Sims & Jefferies; Worby, William*

OSTRICH INN
Overlooking the Orwell at the foot of Bourne Hill and close to Bourne Bridge, which crosses Orwell Creek, is a hostelry which for many years bore the sign of an ostrich with a horseshoe in its beak. It is said to have been built in 1612, three years after Sir Edward Coke, the Chief Justice, had acquired the manor of Bourne Hall, on whose lands it was sited. Sir Edward's crest was an ostrich, heraldically depicted holding a horseshoe in its beak, an allusion to the legendary wide-ranging diet of this bird. The historian G.R. Clarke

Bourne Bridge and the Ostrich Inn seen across Ostrich Creek. The old bridge shown here still exists but the road now runs over a modern bridge erected alongside it, and the Ostrich is known as The Oyster Reach.

refers to the view from the Ostrich's gardens of the town and the river, a view depicted in Clarke's history of the town in the frontispiece by Henry Davy of *Ipswich from the Ostrich*. The landlord presumably did very well when Jabez Bayley launched the East Indiaman *Orwell* from his Halifax yard in August 1817, since 20,000 people are said to have watched the launch, not a few of them from his premises. When this house changed hands in 1996 the company that acquired and extended it changed the name to The Oyster Reach, under a misapprehension that the name referred to oyster layings in the Orwell.

☛ *See also Oyster fishery; Shipyards*

OYSTER FISHERY

There were oysters in the Orwell for many centuries, which were cultivated well into the twentieth century. Pits in which the shellfish were put for cleansing before being sent to market were to be seen at Fagbury until the Felixstowe container terminals were extended upriver in recent years. The fishery was owned by Ipswich Corporation, which leased it from time to time to the fishermen working the oyster beds. In 1733 the corporation paid 15s. (75p) to Anthony Capon 'for casting brass assizes of oysters for the use of the Corporacion'. These indicated the minimum size of oysters that might be landed and sold. A recurring problem was the dredging of immature oysters and spat (the oyster spawn) by unlicensed fishermen, including piratical fishermen from other rivers; in December 1809 the Treasurer of the Corporation paid Simon Jackaman his fees for taking action against twelve people 'for having dredged in the River Orwell and taken away the oyster spat'. The oyster fishery continued to operate until 1939, when wartime regulations prevented access to the oyster beds between Pin Mill and Shotley. By the end of the war the oysters had largely disappeared.

☛ *See also Ostrich Inn*

PALACE SKATING RINK

When it was opened by the Mayor on 22 March 1909 on the site of the provision market in the Old Cattle Market, this was described as 'the largest and best skating rink in the Eastern Counties'. It was managed by Douglas F. Bostock, owner of the Hippodrome in St Nicholas Street. The fashion for roller skating was short-lived, and by 1912 the rink had become the Palace Electric Theatre. The building was sold in 1920 and the site cleared for the Post Office Sorting Office.

PALMER, HENRY

When the 'Dock Committee' was set up to gather information on the possible provision of a wet dock in 1836 they went to Henry Palmer, vice-president of

the Institution of Civil Engineers and a prominent London consulting engineer, a man at the top of his profession. The scheme he put forward, which seems to owe a good deal to the ideas of William Chapman more than thirty years earlier, was to block off a part of the river with dams top and bottom to form a wet dock and to cut a bypass channel to carry the water of the River Gipping. The big difference was that Chapman proposed an eleven-acre dock, whereas Palmer was suggesting one three times that size, far larger than anything then existing on the Thames, Humber or Mersey. Palmer also designed timber-framed warehouses, built out at first-floor level over the quay so that the front wall was above the quayside. He stated in his report that 'it is proposed to support the front walls of the warehouses upon a Colonnade, the Columns being composed of Cast Iron'. Those handsome warehouses have gone, but the cast-iron columns remain. Last-minute attempts to persuade the promoters to 'throw the Dock Bill overboard into Deep Water' failed. On 30 June 1837 the Ipswich Dock Act received Royal Assent, just ten days after Victoria's accession to the throne. Now Palmer's scheme would enable Ipswich to compete with other east coast ports in the new era of trade and industrial expansion.
☛ *See also* **Wet Dock**

PAUL, R. & W.
Established in Ipswich in 1850 by Robert Paul (1806–1864), the family firm of maltsters, corn merchants and manufacturers of animal feed stuffs was built up by his sons Robert (1844–1909) and William (1850–1928). The brothers also became shipowners and bargeowners, with a fleet of vessels to bring in their raw materials, largely from the London docks, and to distribute their products. The last-but-one sailing barge built in Ipswich was the *Jock*, launched by Orvis & Fuller in 1908, which was named after William Paul's grandson and spent some sixty years in the company fleet. The firm continued to use barges to bring barley from London Docks and to carry away malt until about 1970, though by then the barges had been fitted with motors and had lost their sails. Pauls Malts Ltd still had maltings in Ipswich until 2004, but the head office is now at Bury St Edmunds; the animal-feed side of the business, BOCM Pauls, was acquired in 1998 by Greencore, a Dublin-based agri-conglomerate.
☛ *See also* **Malting; Sprittie**

PEASANTS' REVOLT
The causes of the revolt of 1381 were complex: opposition to the poll tax was only one factor. The Statute of Labourers – by which the government attempted to control wages – was widely resented, social changes since the Black Death had created dissatisfaction with the status quo and many country folk wanted to break the hold of the manorial lords over their villein tenants. In spite of the revolt's popular name, its leaders in Suffolk were men

far superior to the labouring class. In Ipswich the rebellion was proclaimed by Thomas Sampson, a well-to-do yeoman of Harkstead and Kersey, and he was supported by Richard Tollemache of Bentley, from a Norman family that had settled in England well before the Norman Conquest. Another leading rebel was John Battisford, the parson of Bucklesham.

Their targets were the agents of government taxation in Ipswich and representatives of the feudal lords whose efforts to retain control caused such anger among the working people. The rebels ransacked the houses of John Cobat, a burgess and the town's representative in Parliament in 1377, who had collected the first instalment of the poll tax, and John Gerard, another burgess and MP in 1377, who was a wealthy parishioner of St Lawrence's. In Suffolk, the abbeys of Bury St Edmunds and Ely were among the most prominent feudal lords; the rebels murdered William Fraunceys, who may have been an official of St Etheldreda's liberty (Ely Abbey), and attacked the archdeacon's house, although the archdeacon was the non-resident Cardinal of St Angelo. They also robbed the rectory of John, the parson of St Stephen's, because he supported the hated chief justice, Sir John Cavendish. The latter met his death in West Suffolk, given away by a girl who recognised him as he tried to cross a ferry. The Earl of Suffolk, soon involved in putting down the revolt, had his house at Hollesley attacked and the court rolls of his manors, including Wicks Ufford in Ipswich, were burned. The destruction of court rolls was often used to resist manorial control.

The town centre as it was in the 1770s, shown on Joseph Pennington's map. The Market Cross can be seen on Cornhill, and Dr Coyte's garden can be seen north of Boat Lane, later known as Friars Street.

PENNINGTON, JOSEPH

The best idea of Ipswich as it used to be is perhaps to be gained from Joseph Pennington's map of the town, published in 1778. Pennington, who came from Needham Market, was a surveyor who travelled all over the country measuring and mapping land for enclosure. He acted as an Enclosure Commissioner in Derbyshire, Gloucestershire and Wiltshire. He gave notice in the *Ipswich Journal* in 1777 that he was working on a map 'In which will be delineated not only the streets, lanes, public buildings and bounds of the parishes, but likewise the plan of every private building, yard and garden', at half a guinea (52½p.). The map shows a town almost entirely contained within the medieval bank and ditch, with little more than the extra-mural parishes of St Matthew, St Margaret, St Helen and St Clement, and the hamlets of Wykes Bishop and Wykes Ufford, showing any signs of urban expansion outside the 'walls'.

☛ *See also* **Ipswich Journal;** *Ogilby, William*

PICTURE HOUSE

'Moving pictures' were still a novelty when the Picture House in Tavern Street was opened in 1910 by British Cinematograph Theatres Ltd, a national company then expanding in the provinces. Perhaps to compete with the local newsreels at Poole's Picture Palace, the company showed *The Handymen*, a film of life at Shotley Barracks, the Royal Navy's boy training establishment that had been housed in the battleship HMS *Ganges* and was later named *Ganges*. The Picture House was intended to be a cut above other cinemas, meant 'to place before the people of Ipswich a refined form of entertainment, both interesting and instructive, and entirely devoid of anything vulgar' as the press statement said. They underlined this by inviting the curator of the Ipswich Museum, Frank Woolnough, to open the cinema; later he pioneered special film showings in the Picture House to supplement schools' natural history lessons.

Unlike cinemas in converted buildings, the Picture House had been designed from the outset for showing films, by Frank Matcham, a famous theatre architect also responsible for the Hippodrome in St Nicholas Street. It had an associated tea room and restaurant, Jacobean in design, intended to attract shoppers and visitors as well as those at 'the pictures'. The Picture House was enlarged in 1922 and 1927, after which it could seat 1,100 people. It closed in 1958 and was demolished to make way for a branch of Timothy Whites (now Boots)

See Stephen Peart, *The Picture House in East Anglia* (Terence Dalton, 1980)
☛ *See also* **Museum, The Ipswich;** *Poole's Picture Palace*

POOLE'S PICTURE PALACE

Charles W. Poole's 'Myriorama', an entertainment using a series of pictures on a continuous cloth wound on two rollers, came to the Public Hall in about

1900; the scenes were unrolled as a lecturer told the story. From about 1902 Poole added cinematograph shows, thus opening the era of the cinema in Ipswich. Later Poole moved his visiting shows to the Mechanics' Institute Lecture Hall in Tower Street, and in 1909 John R. Poole took a one-year lease of the hall, which opened as the town's first cinematograph theatre, known for many years as Poole's Picture Palace. Part of the early shows consisted of lantern slides but, as the *East Anglian Daily Times* reported, 'the cinephone, the latest novelty of the kind, also plays a prominent part'. An explanation followed: 'A Gramophone discourses songs of well-known artists whilst they appear in the animated picture, and discs are fitted to the machine and the operator's wheel so that their gestures are in complete unison with the voice as it sings from the 'phone and the audience can imagine that the real live singer is before them. It is a clever invention, and is sure to be a popular feature'. It was.

Before very long the manager of the Picture Palace, A.C. Rogers, had acquired a hand-operated cine camera and was producing local newsreels that attracted audiences. Some of those pioneering newsreels have survived to be added to the East Anglian Film Archive.

The Picture Palace closed as a cinema in 1940, but in 1947 it reopened as the Ipswich Arts Theatre, from which the Ipswich Repertory Company moved to the new Wolsey Theatre; it is now a public house, The Old Rep.

See Stephen Peart, *The Picture House in East Anglia* (Terence Dalton, 1980)
☛ *See also Institute, The Ipswich; Picture House*

PORTMAN ROAD

Built about the same time as Princes Street in the mid-nineteenth century, Portman Road (or Portman's Road as it was originally) ran from Handford Road across the Corporation Marshes, including what had been the Portmen's Marsh, to a junction with Railway Station Road (later renamed as part of Princes Street), thus providing a direct route from the west end of the town to the railway station when that opened in 1860. A meadow south of the junction with Portman's Walk was laid out as a cricket ground, and later became used for football. It is now home to Ipswich Town Football Club, and is known to all as 'Portman Road'. On the north side of Handford Road and running up to Barrack Corner was Mill Lane, later Mill Street; in the 1940s this became the upper part of Portman Road.

☛ *See also Portmen; Football Club, Ipswich Town*

PORTMAN'S WALK

Running west from a junction with Portman Road, Portman's Walk is now known as Alf Ramsey Way, after the famous football manager whose statue stands near the junction. It is unfortunate that the borough council should have chosen this road to be renamed, since the name is at least 300 years old and refers to the twelve portmen appointed under the charter of 1200. 'Portmans Walks' can be seen on Pennington's map of 1778 running westwards from Friars Bridge across the marshes on which the portmen grazed their horses; it is shown bordered by two ditches for part of the way and then fenced. The present road runs past the end of Constantine Road to a junction with West End Road, which ran from Portman Walk to London Road; in the 1980s when new traffic schemes were being implemented it was extended to Chancery Road, formerly a muddy cul-de-sac beside the Princes Street maltings.

☛ *See also Portmen*

PORTMEN

Under the charter given to Ipswich by King John in 1200, the government of the town was placed in the hands of two bailiffs and four coroners, the first of whom were elected at a meeting in the churchyard of St Mary-le-Tower on 29 June 1200. At that gathering the inhabitants decided to elect twelve 'capital portmen ... as there are in other free boroughs of England'. The portmen were chosen by a panel of electors, four from each of the town's parishes, at a further meeting on 2 July. The portmen elected that day were the two bailiffs, John fitzNorman and Robert Belines, who were also coroners, the two other coroners, Philip de Porta and Roger Lew, and Amise Boll, Peter Everard, Sayer fitzThurstan, William Gostalk, John le Mayster, Robert Parys, Andrew Peper and John St George. From that time on, their numbers were made up from time to time by election. The Portmen were granted a meadow called Odenholm or Oldenholm on which to keep their horses; in later days it became known as Portmen's Marsh, and is commemorated in Portman Road and the former Portman's Walk.

In the seventeenth century, royal interference began to whittle away at the independence of chartered boroughs, and also created a degree of confusion that began a long process of decline in the town government of Ipswich. In 1665 Charles II, the 'Merry Monarch', granted a charter under which the portmen and the twenty-four councilmen themselves chose men to fill their ranks as the holders of these posts died. There arose a struggle between the portmen and 'the Twenty-four', a struggle intensified in the eighteenth century when the division became a political one. The portmen were all Whigs or 'Yellows', while the Twenty-four were all Tories or 'Blues', and for the most part the interests of the two political parties took precedence over the interests of the town. Some members of the corporation flagrantly disregarded not only the town's best interests but their own duty: in 1702 Richard Phillips was fined the very large sum of £100 for neglecting his duties as a portman, and the next year a number of townsmen were fined for neglect of duty or for refusing to serve, Henry Sparrowe being fined £20 and discharged from his office of portman 'for non-attendance and neglect of duty'.

Small wonder that in 1835 it was remarked that some of those chosen were 'ill qualified for the office' and that the town authorities enjoyed neither the confidence nor the respect of the inhabitants. It had been the custom to choose new portmen from the ranks of the Twenty-four, and a low point was reached when the portmen, every one a 'Yellow', refused to appoint any new portmen since it would mean choosing men of the opposing political persuasion. This led to a gradual reduction in the ranks of the portmen, and by 1820 there were only four left. It was then discovered that four could not be considered a majority of the Twelve and that, since a majority was needed to elect new portmen, none could be chosen. It seemed that the portmen were doomed to extinction after more than six hundred years. As it happened, the corporation was dissolved by the Municipal Reform Act of 1835. It was succeeded by a new corporation consisting of mayor, aldermen and councillors.

☛ *See also Bailiffs; Charter; Freemen*

POTTERIES, THE

A name given to the area south of Rope Walk that was developed in the nineteenth century by speculative builders, with little terrace houses for the growing population drawn by the town's engineering works. It took its name from the Rope Walk Pottery occupied in the 1860s by George Schulen, who described himself as 'manufacturer of Glazed Pipes and every description of Brown Earthenware'. The housing was poorly built and, because of the old claypits on which it was sited, very soon began to settle. Many houses were in multiple occupation, and as the population boomed they became increasingly overcrowded. In a report to the town council Dr George Elliston, the town's first Medical Officer of Health, wrote of individual rooms in 'old and dilapidated houses' let out to families who were forced to live, cook, eat and sleep in just the one room. Dr Elliston remarked on the considerable profits for a proprietor who paid £10 per annum for a five-room house and let each of those rooms at up to 4s. 6d. a week. The whole area was cleared in the first half of the twentieth century, and the Suffolk College now stands on part of the site.

See Frank Grace, *The Late Victorian Town* (Phillimore, Chichester, 1992)

PRETTY, WILLIAM, & SONS

Corset-making was a local industry in the early nineteenth century, with many women carrying on the trade in their own homes. The firm of Footman, Pretty & Nicholson opened a factory at Sudbury, and then in

1881–2 built a very large factory in Tower Ramparts, Ipswich, which at its peak employed well over a thousand workers, mainly women. William Pretty took over the corset-making side of the business in 1889 and it operated for many years under that name. In the very early years of the twentieth century, when such provision for women workers was virtually unheard of, the firm provided a crèche for young mothers employed at Tower Ramparts; it is not known how long this continued. At that period William Pretty & Son had smaller production units in Stowmarket, Sudbury, Bury St Edmunds, Diss, Hadleigh and Beccles. The business was reconstructed under new control in 1930 and the company then began large-scale production of artificial silk underwear.

A booklet published by the firm in 1938 says that 'the production of artificial silk underwear which in 1930 was some 500 dozens per week, has now reached the imposing figure of 1,000 dozens a day, which is probably the biggest production of this class of goods, not only in this country, but in the world'. As a result the number of staff rose from 350 in 1930 to 1,300 in 1938. Several generations of some families worked in the Tower Ramparts factory and the memories of former employees are of strict discipline but also a very happy atmosphere; the annual coach outing to Clacton or some other

The William Pretty corset and underwear factory in Tower Ramparts before demolition in the 1980s. At one time it employed more than a thousand workers.

seaside resort is recalled with affection. The company was taken over by Courtaulds in 1968, after which the number of workers was considerably cut. Tower Ramparts closed in 1982, production being transferred to much smaller premises on the Hadleigh Road Industrial Estate.
☛ *See also Footman, Pretty & Co; Staymakers*

PRINCES STREET
Although this street named after Prince Albert now runs from Cornhill to the railway station, it was developed in several sections. It was originally intended to run only from the Cornhill to Friars Bridge, roughly where the Greyfriars roundabout is now. Even this much was unfinished when the railway station opened in 1860 and a timber bridge was thrown across the river to carry the new Railway Station Road. This ran across the Corporation Marshes and linked the station with Princes Street and what was known as Birds Garden. Princes Street was still incomplete when William Hunt produced his *Descriptive Handbook of Ipswich* in 1864; he describes it as looking 'very much like what it is – a street bored through a mass of houses, gardens, streets and lanes diagonally, leaving corners and angles of old buildings, dead walls with the marks upon them of gable ends dislodged, and bits of lanes running off at curious tangents'. In the course of time, the name Princes Street became applied not only to Railway Station Road but also to that part of King Street running up to Cornhill.
☛ *See also Cornhill*

PROMENADE, THE
Many a picture postcard of bygone Ipswich portrays the Promenade, a much-loved amenity for generations of townspeople, who would spend their Sunday

Although apparently deserted in this Edwardian postcard view, the Promenade was a popular haunt of Ipswich people, particularly at weekends when they walked between the trees beside the New Cut and viewed the ships in the Dock.

mornings strolling under the lime-trees alongside the New Cut and looking at the vessels in the dock. Laid out in the 1840s as part of the Wet Dock project, the Promenade stretched from the original entrance lock to the lower dam, site of the new entrance constructed in 1879–81; at the latter end were a cottage for 'the keeper of the Promenade', a shelter (known to everyone as The Umbrella) and a large statue of a winged horse. In 1912 the Dock Commission planned to end the public right-of-way along the Promenade, and though the war in 1914 meant those plans were not carried into effect the Promenade eventually disappeared under railway lines. Nobody seems to have protested when the Dock Commission applied for the Act of Parliament that gave them powers to close the Promenade, but its loss has remained a matter of public regret ever since.

☛ *See also Dock Commissioners; Umbrella, The;Wet Dock*

PURDIS FARM

To the east of Ipswich between the Felixstowe and Buckleshawe roads is an area known as Purdis Farm, which was at one time extra-parochial: it belonged in no parish. At the time of Domesday Book, however, there was a church of St Petronille and the historian G.R. Clarke tells us that 'in the year 1546, when the doctrines of the Reformation were making great progress, it is stated that the image of St Christopher, near Sudbury, and the image of St Petronille, near Ipswich, were demolished and destroyed'. Clarke also records a grant from Charles II allowing the Corporation of Ipswich to shoot cormorants 'in the woods hereabout' which had, he said, led to the virtual extermination of the birds. St Petronille is said to have been the daughter of St Peter; her skull was kept at Bury Abbey and taken into the fields at appropriate times to protect the crops from disease.

The area is now occupied by a Sainsbury supermarket and modern housing; during the laying out of the housing estate in 2002, an archaeological excavation revealed an extensive Anglo-Saxon cemetery. The origin of the name is obscure: Norman Scarfe says in his *Shell Guide to Suffolk* that the name is derived from St Petronille, but it may be that at some time it was simply Mr Purdy's Farm.

PYKENHAM'S GATEHOUSE

William Pykenham was a fifteenth-century Archdeacon of Suffolk, one of the dignitaries who controlled areas of the Norwich diocese for the bishop, and from 1472 onwards he was also Dean of Bocking, the title given to the incumbent of Hadleigh. The brick gateway that he built about 1471 as an entrance to the archdeacon's house still stands in Northgate Street, and is now the home of the Ipswich Building Preservation Trust. Apart from the imposing brick front and side walls of the archway, the structure is timber-

The gateway built in 1471 for the archdeacon's house in Northgate Street.

framed with wattle-and-daub filling between the studs. The room over the archway accommodated the gatekeeper and his family. The exterior of the timber-framed upper storey was rendered over, probably very early in the nineteenth century, but the timbers were exposed as part of the restoration carried out in 1983 by the Ipswich Building Preservation Trust. Proof that the frame was intended to be exposed is provided by the moulded collars and bressumers and by the precision of the studwork. There is also significant carving in the spandrels and on the stub corner-post. Soon after finishing the gateway to his Ipswich house, Pykenham set about building the massive Deanery gateway in Hadleigh, completed by 1495; the projected Deanery itself was never built, and by 1497 Archdeacon Pykenham himself was dead.
☛ *See also Building Preservation Trust, Ipswich*

QUADLING STREET
Now lost to the development of Cardinal Park, Quadling Street took its name from coachbuilder Edwin Quadling whose quite extensive premises stood on the corner of that street and Wolsey Street in the 1840s. For a time Quadling was in partnership with William Catt, who had taken over the family coachbuilding business in St Matthew's from his uncle Samuel in 1840, and the firm of Catt & Quadling contracted to build a number of second-class carriages and coal wagons for the Eastern Union Railway. Unhappily, one of their carriage-building shops in Handford Road collapsed during a gale in February 1847, doing some £700 worth of damage to the EUR coaches

inside. At the end of that year the partnership was dissolved: Catt took over his former partner's coachbuilding business and 'Quadling & Company' took over the Quadling Street/Wolsey Street property, soon linked to the dock tramway by a curved siding whose trackbed survived as a footpath until about 1980. Another gale blew down part of the works in 1850. Quadling was declared bankrupt not long afterwards, and at the hearing the Commissioner remarked on his premises having twice been blown down: 'Either he must have been a very odd kind of builder, or Ipswich must be a very stormy place.' The site of the carriage works was taken over by E.R. & F. Turner for their Greyfriars Works.

On the corner of Quadling Street and Cecilia Street was the depot of the Ipswich horse tramway. On the coming of the electric trams, the depot with its stables and car shed was sold to a haulage contractor, who used it until the site was cleared for the building of Cardinal Park. The tram rails survived in the yard almost to the end of the twentieth century.

See Hugh Moffat, *East Anglia's First Railways* (Terence Dalton, 1987)
☛ *See also Railway, Eastern Union; Trams, Horse; Turner, E.R. & F.*

RACECOURSE

For at least two hundred years Ipswich had its own racecourse on heathland between the Felixstowe and Nacton roads. The Races were held each June from at least 1710 and were frequented by the gentry of south-eastern Suffolk and officers of the cavalry regiments stationed at Ipswich Barracks and elsewhere. Ipswich Races acquired a certain status when in 1727 they were allocated a Royal Plate worth 100 guineas (£105). There were not many races each year, but each race was run in several heats over the 2½-mile course; any horse failing to reach a 'distance post' by the time the winner passed the winning post 240 yards ahead was 'distanced' and barred from further heats.

In the early days, the gentry simply drove up in their carriages and parked beside the course, while the 'lower classes' gathered in groups alongside and sometimes spilled over on to the course itself, causing problems for the riders. In 1775, 'a substantial gallery' was erected beside the course. The following year a covered stand was added; over it in golden letters was the inscription 'The Gentlemen's Stand'. Admission to the gallery was just sixpence, but places in the Gentlemen's Stand cost a half-crown, or 2s. 6d. (12½p), a sum that successfully excluded 'the lower sort'. Apart from the racing, there were sideshows of various kinds as well as refreshment booths selling drinks, mainly intoxicating ones. In 1795 the principal sideshow was a menagerie, including an elephant; admission to this menagerie was a shilling, but servants were allowed in at half-price, presumably when accompanying their masters.

Although the last steeplechase was run in 1895, flat racing went on until 1911. Seven years later the town council decided to build a housing estate on the land, using a striking layout evident to anyone flying from the nearby Ipswich Airport: a number of long, straight roads met at a focal point, which served as the hub of a road forming three-quarters of a circle. The first houses on the estate were occupied in 1921.

RAGGED SCHOOL

In the mid-nineteenth century, parts of Ipswich were inhabited by 'a class of boys and girls who are prevented, either by their debased condition, by the worthlessness or criminality of their parents, or the tattered state of their garments, from receiving instruction at any previously existing school'. In 1849 Richard Dykes Alexander, the Quaker banker and philanthropist, set up the Ipswich Ragged School for such children, in a cottage in St Clement's Church Lane. The school later moved to purpose-built premises in Waterworks Street and came under the influence of Joshua George Newman, who for nineteen years taught probably the most difficult and intractable pupils that any schoolmaster ever had to deal with. With the help of his wife Deborah and a few volunteers, Newman taught these unruly youngsters not only to read and write but to chop firewood and to work at carpentry. In 1859 he was said to have been coping single-handed with 135 children, who received 'the best instruction it is possible for one master to impart to so many'. When the Ipswich School Board came into being in 1871 under the provisions of the 1870 Forster Education Act, subscriptions to the Ragged School dried up; the building became the first board school, known as Waterworks Street Infants. It

The premises of the old Ragged School survive in Waterworks Street, many years after the school itself came to an end.

was soon handed back to its owners, who continued to minister to the poorest of the town's children for many more years, though only in the evenings and on Sundays. New premises were built in Bond Street in the early twentieth century; both those and the Waterworks Street school building still exist, though put to other uses.

☛ *See also Alexander, Richard Dykes*

RAILWAY, EASTERN UNION

When the Eastern Counties Railway, of which John Cobbold and his son John Chevallier Cobbold were directors, ran out of money after reaching Colchester and declared that the line would stop there, the Cobbolds set up the Eastern Union Railway Company to bring the railway on to Ipswich. The new company was almost entirely promoted and initially financed from Ipswich. The engineer was Peter Bruff, who had trained under Joseph Locke. The station was in Croft Street, near the south end of the tunnel that was to carry the railway on to Bury St Edmunds and Norwich. The official opening of the Colchester–Ipswich line took place on 11 June 1846, which was declared a general holiday in Ipswich by the Mayor, and the first train was greeted at Ipswich by 600 ladies waving 'snowy kerchiefs'. The formal opening of the line to Bury followed on 7 December, but it was not until 1849 that the line reached Norwich.

Ipswich was now connected to the rail network, but the Eastern Counties Railway refused to co-operate in any way and resorted to such tricks as sending off the London train five minutes ahead of the arrival of the Eastern Union train from Ipswich. Completion of the Eastern Union line to Norwich provoked further hostility from the Eastern Counties, which had a line from London to Norwich by way of Cambridge and was determined not to allow a competitor to interfere with traffic on that route. The war between the two companies continued until 1854, when the Eastern Counties took over the running of the Eastern Union lines; it might have seemed like defeat for the Ipswich interest, but Bruff became engineer and superintendent of the Eastern Union section of the Eastern Counties Railway and then, in November 1854, assumed responsibility for the whole system. In 1862 the Eastern Counties, and with it the Eastern Union section, became a part of the Great Eastern Railway.

See Hugh Moffat, *East Anglia's First Railways* (Terence Dalton, 1987)

☛ *See also Bruff, Peter; Cobbold, John; Cobbold, John Chevallier*

RAILWAY ENGINEERING

☛ *See Ransomes & Rapier; Ransomes, Sims & Jefferies*

RAMSEY, SIR ALF
☞ *See Football Club, Ipswich Town*

RANSOME & CO
A firm of agricultural and general engineers set up in Ipswich by Robert Ransome in 1789 and known in 1809 as Ransome & Son, in 1818 Ransome & Sons, from 1825 J. & R. Ransome, from 1830 J.R. & A. Ransome, from 1846 Ransomes & May, from 1852 Ransomes & Head, from 1869 Ransomes, Sims & Head and from 1884, Ransomes, Sims & Jefferies Ltd. Over the years it not only developed an extensive export trade in agricultural implements but also diversified into civil engineering, railway engineering, and the manufacture of lawnmowers, grass machinery and electric vehicles, including trolleybuses.
☞ *See also Orwell Works; Ransome, James; Ransome, Robert; Ransomes & Rapier; Ransomes, Sims & Jefferies*

RANSOME, JAMES (1782–1849)
Indentured to his father at Ipswich as a young man, James later moved to Yarmouth to set up his own business there. He returned to Ipswich in 1813 to become his father's partner, bringing with him some of his best workmen, and the Ipswich firm then became Ransome & Son. Five years later his younger brother Robert also became a partner. When Robert, senior, retired from the business in 1825 it became known as J. & R. Ransome.

James Ransome's son **James Allen Ransome (1806–1875)** also joined the firm, becoming a partner in 1830, at which time the title changed again to J. R. & A. Ransome. In the course of his work James Allen gained a specialised technical knowledge of agricultural engineering, and his expertise was important to the business in developing the agricultural implements section of their trade. In 1843 he published *The Implements of Agriculture*, which has been described as the best treatise on implements and machinery before the age of steam.
☞ *See also Orwell Works; Ransome & Co; Ransome, Robert; Ransomes, Sims & Jefferies*

RANSOME, ROBERT (1753–1830)
The founder in 1789 of the firm that eventually became Ransomes, Sims & Jefferies, Robert Ransome was the son of a Wells schoolmaster, Richard Ransome, and was apprenticed to a Norwich ironmonger. After coming out of his indentures he set up his own foundry near Whitefriars Bridge in Norwich, and in 1785 took out a patent for tempered cast-iron ploughshares. In 1789 he made a momentous decision to move from Norwich to Ipswich, taking with him his young family and a single workman, Thomas Rush. The

foundry he set up in St Margaret's Ditches, on the inside of the town ramparts, was the start of a great and long-lasting business which developed from making agricultural implements into civil and railway engineering. His business was based on the Quaker principles of fair dealing and reliability. It is said that the move from Norwich was financed by his own savings of £100 and a loan of a similar sum from a fellow Quaker, the Norwich banker Richard Gurney.

In 1803 Robert Ransome patented the chilled-iron ploughshare, which in practice was self-sharpening; the discovery of the chilling process is, rightly or wrongly, attributed to an accidental spillage of molten iron in the old foundry. In 1808 he took out a further patent for the standardisation of plough parts made of cast iron.

Robert Ransome had two sons, James and Robert, who both entered the business. He retired in 1825 and died in 1830, being buried in the Quaker burial ground attached to the Friends' Meeting House in College Street, Ipswich, demolished in 1995. The grave is now obliterated, and unmarked.

☞ *See also Orwell Works; Ransome & Co; Ransome, James; Ransomes, Sims & Jefferies*

RANSOMES & RAPIER

This company was formed in 1869 to take over the railway engineering business of Ransomes, Sims & Head, so the parent company could expand its production of agricultural implements. Ransomes & Rapier later diversified into making sluice gear, large cranes – including the biggest of railway breakdown cranes, with capacities of more than 100 tons – and the first cement-mixer lorries. The firm's expertise in locomotive turntables was

A giant walking dragline built by Ransomes & Rapier for the opencast mining of iron ore.

put to a different use in 1904 when a revolving stage was made for the London Coliseum Theatre; sixty years later the firm designed and built a revolving restaurant for the Post Office Tower in London.

The firm made its name also in water control, largely as a result of the invention in 1874 of the Stoney Sluice, of which the firm were the original patentees and manufacturers. In this sluice, the excessive sliding friction created by the pressure of water on the gate was reduced by the fitting of roller bearings between the gate and its abutments. Early installations in Britain and in connection with the first Niagara hydro-electric power station in America were followed in 1902 by sluice gates for the first Aswan Dam on the Nile. Ransomes & Rapier was well known for its work in water control and irrigation in developing countries until a takeover by Newton Chambers led to a transfer of this work to their Sheffield works.

Having begun by building cranes for railway work, the firm went on to build cranes for many other purposes, including steam and electric cranes for cargo handling and for specialist purposes. One of these was a 30-ton crane used in the construction of the breakwater for Dover harbour. At the other end of the scale the firm developed a petrol-electric mobile crane on rubber tyres, with a cantilever jib and a patented variable-voltage speed control system; the first appeared at the British Empire Exhibition at Wembley in 1923. Over the next half-century Ransomes & Rapier developed a whole range of mobile cranes that were even seen on British aircraft carriers during the Second World War.

After that war, the company designed and built a massive walking dragline for removing the overburden from the Northamptonshire ironstone beds. The machine, which weighed 1,400 tons and could dig to a depth of 100ft (30m), was supplied to Stewart & Lloyds, who before the war had bought faceshovels made at Waterside Works to do a similar job. The biggest walking draglines, so called because they moved on enormous feet, were the two Rapier W1800 draglines, one of which went to the National Coal Board for opencast mining in South Wales; the other was exported to Italy, where it was used for stripping marl and shale overburden from lignite coal seams. The W1800 was reputed to be the largest walking dragline in the world.

Ransomes & Rapier were early in the field with cement-mixers, some of the early models being powered by steam engine, and in 1932 they were the first in Britain to manufacture mixers mounted on lorries, an innovation that revolutionised the building and civil engineering trades. The firm also developed pumps that could deliver concrete from the lorry to anywhere on site.

Sadly the Ipswich company fell into the hands of Robert Maxwell. Waterside Works was closed and demolished, the site being of more importance to the new owner than the loss of employment and the ending of a long tradition. That tradition is still celebrated at the Ipswich Transport Museum at Priory Heath, where an annual reunion is held for former employees of the company.

☛ *See also China, First railway in; Ransomes, Sims & Jefferies; Rapier, Richard Christopher*

RANSOMES, SIMS & JEFFERIES

Founded in 1789 by Robert Ransome, Ransomes began life as general ironfounders in premises close to the river and opposite St Mary-at-the-Key Church. In his first advertisement after moving to Ipswich, published in the *Ipswich Journal* on 18 April 1789, Robert Ransome offered to 'Manufacture, to Pattern or Drawing, plain & ornamental gates, pallisadoes, cast Iron work for tombs, stair cases, &c. Also, Bath stoves, kitchen ranges, with oven, heater & stewing stoves, kitchen & stove backs, furnace bars, sash & scale weights, plough & barrow wheels, breasts and ground irons, cart boxes, harrow teeth etc. ... ' – in other words, anything the customer might want. How long he remained opposite St Mary-at-the-Key is uncertain, but quite soon the business moved to a former malting in St Margaret's Ditches (now Old Foundry Road), a site his foundry was to occupy for some sixty years.

The emphasis in that first advertisement is somewhat odd in view of the importance that ploughs and other implements assumed in the firm's later operations. Ransome had taken out a patent for improvements in the manufacture of cast-iron ploughshares even before his move to Ipswich, and later took out further significant patents relating to ploughs and ploughshares; it would be true to say that Robert Ransome is remembered for his important contributions to the development of the plough.

The business espoused new technologies with enthusiasm: in 1807 a steam engine erected by a Cornish engineer was set to work in the foundry to operate the bellows for the smithy and to drive other machinery, and five years later the Norfolk-born engineer William Cubitt became engineer to Ransomes, taking the firm into the field of civil engineering. In 1818, when a flood washed away the old Stoke Bridge, Cubitt designed and oversaw the construction of a new cast-iron bridge; though the erection was carried out by Ransomes, the casting was done at Dudley, the ironwork being loaded into canal boats and sent to Gainsborough on the Trent, where it was loaded into a coaster for shipping to Ipswich. Although Cubitt eventually left to become a consulting engineer in London, he seems to have retained links with the Ransomes.

In 1836 a new partner, Charles May, was brought into the business (which continued to trade as J.R. & A. Ransome), and he developed the manufacture of railway materials, a significant branch of work at that time when railways were being constructed the length and breadth of the country and overseas. This

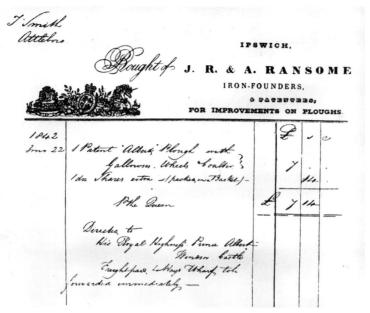

The date is given in the Quaker style on this 1842 invoice for '1 Patent "Albert" Plough with Gallowses' consigned to Prince Albert, the Prince Consort, on the Queen's behalf. At top left is the name of Theophilus Smith, of Attleborough, who had discussed the Ransomes plough with the Prince Consort during a visit to Windsor Castle.

diversification enabled the company to prosper at times when farming was in depression; in many years the railway work formed the greater share of the firm's income. Eventually, a boom in exports of agricultural implements led to the railway department being transferred to a new company, Ransomes & Rapier.

Further diversification resulted from the acquisition of a licence in 1832 to produce lawnmowers invented by Edwin Beard Budding. Although at first only a few mowers were turned out each year, there came a time when Ransomes became one of the three biggest manufacturers of mowers. It was Ransomes who in 1902 built the first commercial motor lawnmower, and they went on to produce electrically-powered mowers as well. In 1914 they built the first of their battery-electric lorries, examples of which are still to be seen at the Ipswich Transport Museum, and in the 1920s they began building trolleybuses, which ran not only in Ipswich but also in Penang and Singapore. They built a variety of small electric vehicles, including fork-lift trucks and tractors for airport use, at the same time that they continued the agricultural tradition by bringing out a range of combine harvesters.

In two world wars Ransomes turned to munitions, playing a very significant part in the war effort; in the First World War one of their workers, Sergeant A.F. Saunders, won the Victoria Cross. After the Second World War the firm moved from the Orwell Works, its home since 1849, to a new works at Nacton. Today the company is American-owned and produces only grass machinery; the agricultural-machinery business was disposed of some years ago.

See Carol and Michael Weaver, *Ransomes 1789–1989 A Bicentennial Celebration* (Ransomes Sims & Jefferies, 1989)

RAPIER, RICHARD CHRISTOPHER (1836–1897)

Born at Morpeth in Northumberland, Richard Rapier was apprenticed at the Newcastle engineering firm of Robert Stephenson & Co after education at Christ's Hospital, London. In 1862 he took up work with Ransomes in Ipswich and for six years was in charge of the Railway Department at Orwell Works. When in 1869 it was decided to hive off the railway business to a new company, Rapier became a partner in the new firm, which supplied a good deal of equipment for narrow-gauge railways in the Welsh slate quarries during the 1870s. In the same period he achieved his ambition of building the first railway in China, between Shanghai and Woosung, at the mouth of the Yangtse. In 1878 he published *Remunerative Railways for New Countries*, in which he advocated the use of narrow-gauge lines in sugar plantations and similar places. He was also a director of the Southwold Railway, opened in 1879, but the popular story that he brought home equipment and engines from Woosung for use on this line has no basis in fact. Rapier took a leading part in making the change from wrought iron to steel structures in railway engineering.

☛ *See also Ransomes & Rapier; China, First railway in*

REAVELL, SIR WILLIAM

Reavell was the patentee with W.H. Scott of a design of totally-enclosed high-speed steam engine, and set up a works in Ranelagh Road on land bought from the Great Eastern Railway in 1898. Many of these highly efficient steam engines were supplied to electricity generating stations, including the Ipswich generating station in Constantine Road, just across the Gipping from the Ranelagh Road works. Reavell & Co Ltd also built air compressors, an early model being the Quadruplex compressor with four radially-disposed cylinders. The first Quadruplex compressor made in Ipswich continued to operate in a paint factory in London until it was put out of action during the Blitz more than forty years later. Few steam engines were built after about 1908, the firm thereafter concentrating on air compressors for a variety of applications. Reavell compressors were installed in Royal Navy submarines to supply compressed air for propelling torpedoes and for emptying the water-ballast tanks when the submarine was required to surface. Sir William Reavell (he was knighted in 1938) played a part in bringing trolleybuses to the streets of Ipswich, his firm supplying the rotary compressors that operated the trolleybus brakes. During the Second World War small compressors were built to charge the hydrogen bottles carried on lorries and trailers for the inflation of barrage balloons used in the Ipswich area and around many other large towns to deter low-level air attack. Special compressors designed for pressures of up to 7,000lb per sq. inch are used in manufacturing expanded rubber, while machines for pressures up to 22,000lb per sq. inch are used for research into plastics and fuels. Compressors of this type were supplied to the Cavendish Laboratories at Cambridge for early work on the structure of the atom. Following amalgamation in 1969 with another well-known firm making compressors, the Ipswich firm is now known as Compair Reavell.

REGIMENT, THE IPSWICH
In 1794 the corporation asked Lord Amherst to suggest to King George III that he grant permission for the raising of an Ipswich Regiment. It was to consist of thirty-two serjeants, thirty corporals, twenty-two drummers and six hundred private soldiers, to aid in the defence of the country against the French. The resolution was sent in writing to Lord Amherst, but the proposal was not taken up.
☛ *See also Barracks; St Helen's Barracks; Stoke Barracks*

REYNOLDS, BERNARD
Born in Norwich in 1915, the sculptor Bernard Reynolds had his studio in Ipswich or in the village of Barham for more than forty years, and was

Lecturer in Charge of Three-dimensional Design at Suffolk College until 1980. He left a rich heritage of sculpture in his adopted town, including a ship sculpture – based on the ship on the borough seal – that won

The Civic Centre with Bernard Reynolds' sculpture, based on the ship borne on the borough seal, standing on a roundabout to the left.

the Sir Otto Beit Medal for Sculpture in 1972; it is now on the Civic Drive roundabout close to the Civic Centre. Outside Suffolk College are two upright features entitled *Pylons* which Reynolds made in 1961 in collaboration with the Ipswich architect Birkin Haward, and in the Wolsey Gardens behind Christchurch Mansion is his *Triple Mycomorph*, commissioned by Tom Gondris as a memorial to his parents.

RITZ, THE
Built on the site of the Waggon and Horses right next to the Ancient House in the Buttermarket, the Ritz cinema was opened by film actress Dame Anna Neagle on 4 January 1937. The first film shown was *The Three Maxims*, appropriately starring Anna Neagle. A feature of the Ritz was the magnificent Wurlitzer cinema organ that rose from a pit in front of the screen at the interval; the organ survived the closure and demolition of the cinema, being installed in an Ipswich church. Towards the end of its life this cinema was renamed the ABC; it closed in 1986 and was demolished to make way for a branch of British Home Stores that moved from the Tavern Street/Tower Street corner.

RIVER COMMISSIONERS
At the end of the sixteenth century, Ipswich was a prosperous town with 'a great trade and … an abundance of rich merchants', but in the seventeenth

The embanked marshes whose creation caused so much silting of the Orwell can be seen on this plan of proposed improvements to the river put forward in 1804.

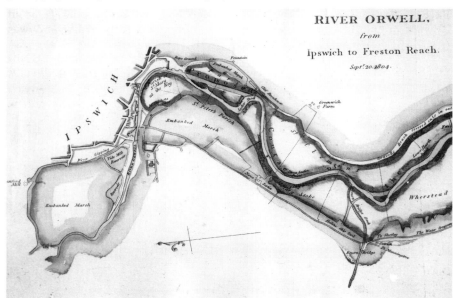

its trade declined when navigation of the river was seriously impeded by silting that resulted from the embanking of marshes near the town. A number of Ipswich merchants and business people got together to call in the engineer William Chapman, who had been making improvements to rivers and constructing canals in various parts of the British Isles. In his first report, made in 1797, Chapman suggested either constructing a ship canal – to bring ships up from Downham Reach along the north side of the Orwell into an eleven-acre dock – or dredging the river, to provide a straighter and deeper channel that would bring ships up to the town quays and also increase the amount of tide in the upper reaches of the river. That would have cost too much for the liking of the merchants and shipowners, and Chapman was forced to scale down his plans several times while would-be improvers prevaricated and the corporation manoeuvred to retain its old rights and privileges. It was only in 1805 that a Bill for 'improving and rendering more commodious the Port of Ipswich' passed through Parliament and received Royal Assent from George III, setting up a body of River Commissioners.

The commissioners bought a steam dredger, only the fourth in Britain. Money to pay for the dredger and other equipment was subscribed by individual commissioners, the Quaker banker Samuel Alexander alone putting up £3,150 in the first year. The dredger – and a group of labourers known as 'the mud men' who waded into the shallows to shovel the mud away – soon made an impact on the navigation, cutting new channels and deepening existing ones, and the first year's loss was turned into a profit in succeeding years. By 1830 the commissioners had not only paid off the original loan of £8,000 but had also managed to accumulate a surplus of £25,000, though in the early years they had led a somewhat hand-to-mouth existence; Robert Cole had resigned as harbourmaster in 1807, eighteen months after his appointment, because he objected to having to pay the labourers' wages out of his own pocket and then having to wait for the commissioners to pay him month by month.

In the 1830s the River Commissioners were seen to have done much to improve the river and to increase the trade of the port. The time had come for another step forward, and a Dock Committee was appointed to investigate the possibility of building a Wet Dock in which vessels might lie afloat at all states of the tide. There were those in the town who opposed such 'extravagance', but the Dock Committee went ahead with the preparation of a Parliamentary Bill that would empower a new body of Dock Commissioners to go ahead with the construction of a dock such as William Chapman had proposed some forty years earlier.

☛ *See also Chapman, William; Dock Commissioners; Wet Dock*

RIVER LADY

During the 1950s a pleasure vessel named *River Lady* ran trips on the Orwell from a berth in the New Cut. She had been built during the Second World War as a naval motor launch of the Fairmile B type and was brought to the Orwell in 1949 by the Devon Star Shipping Company. Her place was later taken by the *River Lady II*, another launch of the same type, operated by the East Anglian Cruising and Ferry Service Ltd. In 2004 a passenger launch, the *Orwell Lady*, was running a similar service from the Wet Dock.
☛ *See also Orwell, River; Wet Dock*

ROBSON, SIR BOBBY
☛ *See Football Club, Ipswich Town*

ROPE WALK

A reminder of the days when the port of Ipswich had a number of ropemakers producing the cordage with which ships were rigged, Rope Walk was originally known as Ropers Lane or Rope Lane. It took its name from a rope walk that ran parallel to the lane on its southern side. In 1625 Thomas Gallant was given the use of 'ropers lane' for ropemaking at an annual rent of ten shillings, and twenty-five years later Frauncis Searle was granted permission to use 'Roaperes Lane' for ropemaking 'as latelie Gallant had the same And under the same yerelie Rent that Gallant pd for the same during the Townes pleasure'.

There were other ropeyards marked on Ogilby's map between 'the way to Brightwell' (Back Hamlet) and 'the way to Nacton and Trimly and ye Fort' (Fore Hamlet), and alongside the river just south of the shipyards in St Clement's parish. The last of the town's rope walks seems to have been that operating on the south side of Felixstowe Road, opposite the end of Newton Road, and seen on Edward White's map of 1867.
☛ *See also Shipyards*

ROSE LANE

Running from St Peter's Street to Turret Lane, Rose Lane took its name from the Rose public house on the St Peter's Street corner. The present name goes back at least to the seventeenth century, but it had an earlier name. Ogilby's map shows it as Cursoms Lane alias Rose Lane; clearly Cursom is derived from Lord Curson, the Count of the Holy Roman Empire, who had had a house nearby in Silent Street.
☛ *See also Curson, Lord; Curson's House*

ROTUNDA, THE

One of the most distinctive of Ipswich buildings, the Rotunda stood at the east side of the Cornhill. It was the brainchild of George Gooding, who

A print of the Rotunda, a market house designed by George Gooding to attract shoppers to its stalls. It failed to do so because he did not provide sufficient ventilation.

designed his circular market house on the model of the Halle au Blé in Paris. The first stone was laid on 10 February 1794 by the bailiffs, John Kerridge and William Norris, and work proceeded so fast that 500 people were able to attend a concert and ball in the building on 12 August that same year. Gooding is said to have been very proud of the fact that the wooden roof and dome structure was assembled and fixed in place without the use of nails; presumably the timbers were made to interlock in some way so that normal fastenings were unnecessary. The central space in which the market traders set out their stalls was surrounded by a ring of butchers' stalls and shops looking outward on to the Cornhill; living accommodation was arranged on two floors behind the shops.

Sadly, this curious building proved a failure. The builder had failed to realise the need for proper ventilation and, even though the residents of eighteenth-century Ipswich were well used to noxious smells they turned up their noses at the stink that greeted them in the Rotunda. In 1810 it was condemned as a public nuisance and was bought by the corporation for demolition.

☛ *See also Cornhill*

ROYAL SHOW

The Royal Agricultural Society of England held its ninety-third show at Ipswich from 3 to 7 July 1934, on land to the east of Crane Hill that now forms part of the Chantry Estate. The show was attended by the Prince of Wales, later King Edward VIII. It was the only time the Royal Show has been held in Ipswich, but it had visited Suffolk once before, in 1867, when it was held at Bury St Edmunds. The corporation extended its trolleybus service along the London Road specially to serve the Royal Show, and ten new double-deck trolleybuses were built by Ransomes, Sims & Jefferies in 1934 to augment the fleet in time for the show.

☛ *See also Trolleybuses*

ST HELEN'S BARRACKS

With the outbreak of the Napoleonic Wars, a hutted camp known as St Helen's Barracks was built on the fringes of the town on both sides of Rushmere Lane, which later became known as Woodbridge Road. Two thousand workmen are said to have been employed erecting the wooden huts, which according to G.R. Clarke cost £200,000; they could house some 8,000 men. An ill-fated expedition to the island of Walcheren in 1809 saw the hutted camp become a military hospital for some of the thousands of troops who contracted 'Walcheren Fever'. When the first batch of ninety-two patients reached Ipswich on 10 September, four of them were dead on arrival. By the end of the year, over 600 men had been sent to Ipswich, and mortality was high, though Dr J.B. Davis, who was posted to the camp as a temporary physician, wrote that 'every patient had a separate bed with comfortable bedclothes, and the attendance was entirely adequate'.

The burial register of St Margaret's Church shows that 218 men died between September 1809 and February 1810. Possibly that was not the full number, because some parts of the camp were in a detached part of St Stephen's parish. The camp closed about 1813, when materials salvaged from demolished buildings were for sale 'in the centre of St Helen's Barracks'. However, some at least of the huts remained for several years, occupied by squatters – who proved a burden on the parishes in which they were living, according to Clarke.

A public house which was named The Blue Posts is said to have originated as the soldiers' canteen. The site of the barracks is no longer apparent, but there remains Parade Road between Belvedere Road and Brunswick Road as a reminder of where the parade ground once was. Before it was extended to meet Cemetery Lane and Tuddenham Road, Belvedere Road was known as Parade Field Terrace; it originally went only from Woodbridge Road to Parade Road.

☛ *See also Barracks; Stoke Barracks*

ST MILDRED'S CHURCH

Although it is not listed in Domesday Book, St Mildred's Church on the Cornhill is thought to have existed in Saxon times. St Mildred was a daughter of Merewalh, a seventh-century ruler of the area now covered by south Shropshire and Herefordshire, and she became abbess of Minster in Kent, between Richborough and Reculver. She died about AD 700 and it is likely that the East Anglian king of that time, Aldwulf, who was her grandfather's nephew, dedicated the Ipswich church to her. The history of the church is obscure, though it was held at one time by the Prior of SS Peter & Paul, who apparently put in a chaplain. Apart from that, all we know for certain is that some time in the fourteenth century St Mildred's ceased to be used as a church and became the seat of local government. An upper floor was inserted, to be used as a meeting place for the Assembly; the lower storey was divided up to form a kitchen, used to prepare the feasts for the merchant guild, and cellarage or storerooms. A brick extension known as the Hall of Pleas was built between 1335 and 1345, one John Deker being appointed to superintend the building work, and other extensions were added later. An external flight of stone steps led to the upper floor. The front of what had been St Mildred's was pulled down in 1812; it was, according to G.R. Clarke, 'a homely,

An old print of the former St Mildred's Church, with an outdoor staircase giving access to the upper floor. It served as a meeting place for the town authorities for many years before being superseded in the nineteenth century.

The Palladian front of the Town Hall that took the place of the former St Mildred's Church.

uncouth specimen of architecture; and the ascent to the spacious apartment where public business was transacted was by a flight of stairs, clumsy, steep, and dangerous'. Much of that front wall must have been near a thousand years old, but 'the materials with which the walls were composed were so tenaciously cemented together, that it was with difficulty they could be razed for the purpose of erecting a new front, which was copied from a design of Palladio, and executed under the direction of Mr Benjamin Catt'. The very last vestiges of St Mildred's vanished in the demolition that preceded the building of the present Town Hall in 1867.

☛ *See also Churches, Lost; Cornhill; Town Hall*

ST NICHOLAS'S CHURCH

Dwarfed by the Greyfriars complex on the other side of Friars Road, the medieval church of St Nicholas now stands on a rather exposed site between the car park of Cromwell Square, Friars Road and Cutler Street; its reflection in the glass walls of the Willis Corroon building is a pleasant feature of this part of town. The three Saxon carvings preserved inside are probably older than the church itself and might have come from All Saints, an early church that was 'ruined and unproductive in 1535'. Made redundant some years ago, St Nicholas's Church is now being converted into a resource and conference centre for the Diocese of St Edmundsbury and Ipswich. The plans have been drawn up by award-winning architect Ken Fisher, who aims to create a flexible space that can accommodate a variety of conferences and exhibitions and also be used for meetings of the Diocesan Synod.

☛ *See also Historic Churches Trust, Ipswich*

SALTHOUSE STREET

The name of this street, running between the Common Quay and Fore Street, is a reminder of the once-important salt trade. Much of the salt brought into the port came from the Tyne. North and South Shields formed the greatest centre in Britain for the manufacture of salt in the early eighteenth century, with almost 200 saltpans in which seawater was evaporated using the cheap local coal. Edward Clarke, who succeeded Robert Hall as occupier of the salt house near the Common Quay, advertised that he was selling 'the best sorts of Refined and Newcastle Salts'. Salt from the Cheshire salt mines was also brought in from the Mersey, the rock salt being used largely for cattle licks and by tanners in the preservation of hides.

Salthouse Street in the 1970s, with the Bull Inn on the left and Brown's timber yard beyond.

SANCTUARY

Criminals were allowed to seek sanctuary from the law in churches in the Middle Ages. One who did was Nicholas Loweband, who had killed in self-defence a man who was pursuing him with intent to slay him, as the scribe set it down. Nicholas fled to the church of St Mary de Cayo (St Mary-at-the-Quay), where he took sanctuary until the following Sunday, when in the presence of the coroners he confessed his crime. He was ordered to make his way to Dover and quit the country within six days.

It was not only those with blood on their hands who might claim sanctuary and be banished. In 1330, Roger the son of William le Shepherd of Stanway in Essex, 'from fear of being arrested' fled to the church of St Augustine 'in the suburb of Ipswich' and there confessed that he was a common sheep-stealer. The coroners' roll records that 'on Friday next before the feast of St James the Apostle … the said thief abjured the kingdom in the presence of the said coroners and had port given him at Dover.'

SHAMBLES, THE

On the south-east side of Cornhill stood the Shambles or butchery, a timber-framed building with an open ground floor, its upper storey carried on

Said to have been 'newly built' in 1378, the Shambles had an open ground floor where the butchers set out their stalls. No doubt the wind blowing through helped to remove any unpleasant smells.

wooden posts and arches. The butchers set out their stalls on the ground floor. It is mentioned in the town records as 'newly built' in 1378, which seems to make nonsense of the legend that it was built by Cardinal Wolsey (d. 1530) or his father, Robert Wolsey. The only known connection with the Wolsey family is an item in the chamberlains' accounts in 1583 recording a payment of 20s. (£1) 'to Mother Wolsey for her paynes in clensinge the Corne Hill, the Butcherage, and the New Keye, for her whole yere's wages'. In that same year of 1583 it was ordered that the Shambles should be 'new builded', oaks being felled at Ulverston Hall, Debenham, for use in the work. The building survived until 1794, when it was demolished to be replaced by the Rotunda, which lasted only sixteen years before being condemned as a nuisance.

Today 'The Shambles' is the name of a semi-detached house in Wherstead Road. Whether it is named after the old butchery or whether the name has another meaning to the occupant is uncertain.

☛ *See also Cornhill; Wolsey, Thomas*

SHANKLAND, COX REPORT
In 1964–5, planning consultants Graeme Shankland and Oliver Cox prepared a survey of the future development of Ipswich, following a government decision to cope with the booming population of London by expanding Ipswich and two other towns. To accommodate 70,000 people by 1981, it was proposed that 1,500 houses should be built each year for twelve years, in addition to the houses needed by local people. Shankland and Cox also proposed further areas of development around Bramford and Belstead, plus the expansion of Needham Market, Stowmarket and Haughley, providing for an eventual population of some 400,000 in a 'development band' running up the Gipping valley. Ipswich would provide the shopping and entertainment centre for the whole conurbation, to be served by an urban motorway running from Claydon through the west of Ipswich to a river crossing close to the Wet Dock and connecting to what is now the A14 to Felixstowe. The report foresaw that Ipswich, advanced to city status, would become 'the most modern city in Britain'. Massive rebuilding of the town centre was envisaged, with a flyover taking the new urban motorway across the Cornhill, but the whole plan crumbled when in 1969 the Minister of Housing and Local Government announced that the government had decided not to go ahead. Ipswich was not to be an overspill town after all.

See *Ipswich from the First to the Third Millennium* (Ipswich Society, 2001)

SHIPWRECKED SEAMEN'S SOCIETY, IPSWICH
The idea behind 'An appeal from the Seamen's Shipwreck Society To the Benevolent Inhabitants of Ipswich and its Vicinity', published in the *Ipswich*

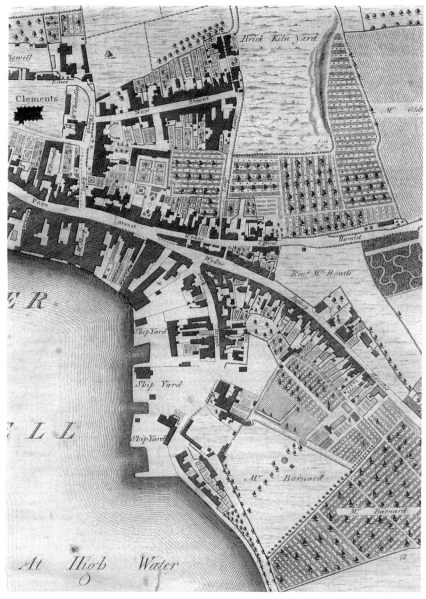

A section of Pennington's map showing the St Clement's shipyards in the eighteenth century, lying between Wykes Bishop Hamlet and the river.

Journal in 1826, was to set up a permanent fund to look after the seamen who subscribed to it, without the fraud so often practised by what we today call conmen. Seamen were to subscribe two shillings each – augmented it was hoped, by donations from the 'Benevolent Inhabitants of Ipswich' – and the relief given to a shipwrecked member would depend on the funds available at the time.

The name of the society was rendered variously in early newspaper reports of anniversary services and dinners, but in later days it was The Ipswich Shipwrecked Seamen's Society, as one can see from the banner carried by members in the anniversary processions. The society broadened its objects to embrace the welfare of the widows and orphans of men who were lost at sea; the banner declared proudly 'Here the Widows & Orphans Find a Friend'. Besides the banner, a feature of the processions was a large model of a three-masted sailing ship named the *Adela* which was carried shoulder-high by two men on a kind of stretcher; that model is now in the Ipswich Museum.

The Ipswich Shipwrecked Seamen's Society continued to do good work well into the twentieth century, although its financial situation could not have been all that good. It operated on quite small subscriptions and collections, which in 1912 totalled only £35 13s. 9½d., including the offertory at the morning and evening services. The society seems to have faded away in the 1930s.

SHIPYARDS

Only one Ipswich shipyard survives, a ship-repair yard operated by George Prior Engineering (Ipswich) Ltd. Tugs, coasters and other vessels are often to be seen hauled out for refitting on the St Clement's Yard patent slip, which consists of a wheeled cradle running on railway lines; the cradle bearing the ship can be hauled out of the water by a powerful electric winch at the head of the slip.

There is now no trace of the yard on which early ships like the 1294 Ipswich galley were built, but it was almost certainly somewhere in St Clement's parish. By the seventeenth century, the principal shipyards were on the east bank below the quays at which vessels loaded and unloaded. As shipbuilding boomed in the eighteenth century, yards were laid out on the other bank, a St Peter's Yard just below Stoke Bridge, another at Nova Scotia and a third at Halifax, near where Ostrich Creek enters the Orwell. Further downriver at John's Ness, just below where the Orwell Bridge now crosses the river, was another shipbuilding site used to build large vessels that could not conveniently be launched from yards in the town.

With the construction of the Wet Dock, the old St Clement's shipyards were required for other purposes, and a new St Clement's Yard was laid out on reclaimed land just outside the dock; the new yard came into operation in

1841. A little more than ten years later a new yard, often referred to as St Peter's Yard, was opened inside the dock, on the 'island' opposite the Customs House, and this yard turned out a succession of vessels for local owners and those in other ports. In the 1860s another yard opened at the Cliff, just below Cobbold's brewery; the site has since disappeared under Cliff Quay.

See Hugh Moffat, *Ships and Shipyards of Ipswich 1700–1970* (Malthouse Press, 2002)

☛ *See also Barnard, John; Bayley, Jabez; Cliff Quay; Galley, the Ipswich; Wet Dock*

SIDEGATE LANE

Running from Humber Doucy Lane to Woodbridge Road, this one-time country lane was used by some travellers as a means of avoiding the Little Yarmouth Turnpike tollgate at what is now the junction of Woodbridge and Rushmere roads. To avoid the loss of tolls the turnpike trustees erected a side gate at the point where the lane met the Woodbridge road, and this side gate gave the lane its name.

SILENT STREET

In the fourteenth century there was open land between the Carmelite priory to the north and the Priory of SS Peter & Paul to the south, which attracted the attention of people seeking to build. In 1333–4 'common soile in

The fine timbered building on the corner of Silent Street is sometimes pointed out as Cardinal Wolsey's birthplace, but in fact he was born on the other side of St Nicholas Street in a building that no longer survives. Today's traffic ensures that Silent Street no longer lives up to its name.

Nicholas parish at the Colehill' was granted to a certain Croxon, the Colehill being a name employed for the whole area between the two religious houses. The name, which seems to suggest an area where coal brought from North-east England by sea was put up for sale, was later given to the thoroughfare that was developed between King Street (later St Nicholas Street) and the Timber Market (later the Old Cattle Market). The name Colehill Lane remained in use throughout the seventeenth century, though an alternative name of Half Moon Street, from a hostelry at the St Nicholas end of the street, was being used towards the end of the century. In the eighteenth century a new name, Silent Street, seems to have taken over. The origin of this new name is something of a mystery, though two possible reasons have been put forward. The first is that the street became unnaturally quiet because of the number of deaths there during the plague outbreak of 1665–6 – one week, 34 out of 64 burials were of plague victims. The other, more likely, explanation is that straw was laid down in the street to quieten the passage of carts and waggons when Curson House was used as a hospital for sick and wounded seamen during the Dutch wars of the 1650s, 1660s and 1670s. If the name indeed originated in the seventeenth century it is a little odd that the earliest known reference to 'Silent Street' is found only in 1764. When the new provision market was opened in 1810 – on a site now occupied by the Buttermarket shopping centre – the street became known for a time as New Market Street, but the new name did not stick. Whatever the origin of the name, for at least 250 years this short thoroughfare has been known to everyone as Silent Street.

☛ *See also Colehill; Curson's House; King's Hospital; Thomas Wolsey*

SIMPSON DIVORCE

An event occurred in Ipswich on 27 October 1936 that had a lasting effect on British history, when Mrs Wallis Simpson was granted a decree *nisi* at the Suffolk Assizes. It led to the abdication of King Edward VIII and the succession of his brother, the Duke of York, as King George VI; had Edward remained on the throne, the story of the Second World War might have been very different.

Mrs Simpson had been living at Beach House, Felixstowe, for some six weeks to establish the residential qualifications for the divorce hearing to be held in Ipswich, which was considered a reasonably out-of-the-way place where the case would attract minimal publicity. Although Beach House had six bedrooms, Mrs Simpson thought it 'tiny' and said there was barely room for her, two companions, and the cook and maid. No doubt the case would have attracted little attention, had it not been for a conversation on a golf course that led to Associated Press of America being told of the pending case. As a result the world's press swarmed into Ipswich for the hearing.

On the day of the hearing the Chief Constable of East Suffolk, George Staunton, took charge of operations aimed at preventing the press from obtaining photographs of Mrs Simpson; although Ipswich had its own borough police force, the County Hall – in which the court was situated – was the headquarters of the East Suffolk force. The police were informed as soon as Mrs Simpson left her temporary home at Felixstowe, and just before she was due to arrive they closed St Helen's Street. Her black Buick, with darkened-glass windows, swept straight along the empty street and turned into the courtyard, the gates being slammed behind it. Mr Staunton took Mrs Simpson to his office to await the hearing. Press photographers had taken up vantage points in buildings in St Helen's and Bond Street, but police raided those various premises and any cameras found were impounded.

The court hearing took just 25 minutes. It was a tense 25 minutes for Mrs Simpson, who recorded later that she was fearful that the judge, Mr Justice Hawke, was determined to deny her the divorce; he appeared to her to be hostile, attempting to discomfit her counsel, Norman Birkitt, KC. The only witnesses were members of the staff from a hotel at Bray-on-Thames, who gave evidence of seeing Mrs Simpson's husband in bed with an unnamed woman who was not Mrs Simpson.

After hearing the evidence the judge said to Mr Birkitt, almost reluctantly according to Mrs Simpson, 'Very well, decree *nisi*.' Mrs Simpson was taken by her solicitor out to the car and the courtroom doors were locked to prevent reporters from leaving. The car sped out of the courtyard gates into Bond Street and was driven away at high speed for London. Pursuit was avoided by a traffic policeman, Sgt Frank Pearl, who drove out after the black Buick, and then spun his police car across the road, effectively blocking it. Those who avoided his blockage found themselves stopped at a 'routine' traffic check on the A12 and asked to show their driving documents.

Even so, within minutes the news was being telephoned not only to Fleet Street newspapers and news agencies but to foreign newspapers, which had been following the royal romance for weeks. The king's wish to marry a divorcee led to a crisis which was only resolved in December 1936 when he announced his abdication; he and Mrs Simpson married in June the following year.

SLADE, SIR THOMAS

Surveyor to the Navy and designer of Nelson's flagship, the *Victory*, Slade was early in his career surveyor on some of the ships built in Ipswich for the Royal Navy. He married an Ipswich woman, Hannah Moore, at Nacton church in 1747; when she died in 1763 she was buried with her parents at St Clement's in Ipswich. When Sir Thomas died at Bath in 1771, his body was brought to Ipswich for burial in St Clement's churchyard; his grave is lost but a memorial was erected in the churchyard in recent years. Slade Street, between Star Lane and Salthouse Street, was named after him in the late twentieth century.

☛ *See also Barnard, John; Shipyards*

SNEEZUMS

For well over a century, the Sneezum family played a significant part in local life as pawnbrokers, making short-term loans on security of anything from a gold watch to a working man's Sunday suit. In the 1890s there were two, Arthur John Sneezum at 35 Elm Street and Henry at 14–18 Fore Street; Henry died about 1905 and the Fore Street business was carried on for a number of years by his executors. By 1925 there were four Sneezums – Arthur John in Norwich Road, another Henry at 89–91 Fore Street, Raymond at 35 Elm Street and William Edward at 14–20 Fore Street – all displaying the three golden balls of the pawnbroker. After the Second World War there were many social changes, and 'Uncle' was much less in demand for the 'popping' of Father's best suit or Mother's flat-iron; the Sneezums adjusted to the changes. A 1949 directory lists Arthur John Sneezum at 31–35 Norwich Road, and Henry and Raymond at 14–20 Fore Street, as jewellers, with Henry as a house furnisher at 89–91 Fore Street; Sneezums Ltd. at 14 High Street had gone upmarket as goldsmiths, silversmiths and jewellers. By 1956 only Raymond at the old premises in Elm Street remained first and foremost a pawnbroker. Henry and Raymond had branched out as photographic specialists, musical instrument dealers, tool merchants and sports outfitters; they also ran a marquee hire service from their premises at the junction of Fore Street and Lower Orwell Street. By the end of the twentieth century all these businesses had gone; but 'Sneezums' is not forgotten in the town.

SOR OF HING

When in 1963 the architects Hare and Pert commissioned Mervyn Crawford to produce a sculpture for their development at the bottom of Berners Street beside the St Matthews roundabout, the design did not meet with universal approval. One reader of the *Evening Star* wrote to the paper saying that it was not the

A sculpture that got its name from a typographical error in a local newspaper.

sort of thing that was wanted in Ipswich. As the letter was being set, the Linotype machine somehow ran out of the letter 't', and the words appeared in the newspaper as 'this sor of hing'. The Sor of Hing it has been ever since.
☛ *See also* **Evening Star**

SPEEDWAY, IPSWICH

Although plans for a speedway track in Bramford Road were turned down because of the effect on a mainly residential area, motor-cycle speedway eventually arrived in Ipswich in 1950 at Foxhall Heath. The track was opened by Group Captain Arthur 'Ben' Franklyn, who had captained Belle Vue in the 1920s and was proud owner of the original Golden Helmet, which he had won in his short career as a rider. He was appointed managing director of the Ipswich Speedway. Nearly twenty years after his last race, he set the first track record of 91.8 seconds at an average speed of 36.54mph. There was further delay when the Speedway Board of Control refused a licence to compete in the third division of the National Speedway because the floodlighting was not ready, but the board did grant an 'open' licence, allowing the club to run a series of non-league events in 1951. The season should have opened with a challenge match between two Second Division teams, Norwich and Southampton, on 24 March 1951; but, just half an hour before the start, heavy rain and snow flooded the circuit and thousands of would-be spectators were turned away. League racing began in 1952, Ipswich having been accepted into the Southern League, but the Witches (as they became known) made an unpromising start, losing a challenge match against Yarmouth 46–38. The Witches have had their ups and downs since then; perhaps the worst year was 1962, which saw the death of Jack Unstead – on Friday 13 April during a home match against Southampton – and the closure of the Foxhall track. It did, however, reopen, and in 1970 there arrived on the scene a man who has perhaps done more for the Witches than anyone else: John 'Tiger' Louis not only as skipper led the Witches to greater things, but in 1973 was awarded the *Speedway Star and News* Personality of the Year award. He is still associated with Ipswich speedway as promoter, and in the team's jubilee year of 2001 took to the track again for a match race with Tony 'Shrimp' Davey.

See Dave Feakes and Colin Barber, *Ipswich Speedway, The First 50 Years* (Feakes & Barber, Ipswich, 2003)

SPILLINGS, JAMES (1825–1897)

Born in Ipswich, James Spilling became an apprentice in the printing office of the *Suffolk Chronicle* and as a young man founded the Ipswich Utilitarian Society, an organisation of which little is remembered. He was an active member of the Chartist movement and a preacher at the Swedenborgian New Jerusalem Chapel in Ipswich. In 1863 he moved to Norwich, where he presumably joined the Swedenborgian congregation of the Catholic Apostolic Church, meeting in St Mary-the-Less in Queen Street.

Today he is remembered for the delightful little books in dialect published by Jarrold & Sons, which sold in their thousands during the later nineteenth century and for some years into the twentieth. *Giles's Trip to London* first appeared with a note addressed to the editor of the *Daily Press*, dated August 1871: 'Mr. Giles Hobbins, who is just returned from a visit to London, has sent for me to write out the story of his adventures. He says he wants the people of these parts to know all about it. He is a good honest fellow, and you may rely on the truthfulness of his tale.' After the tale first appeared in the *Eastern Daily Press*, it was amended to make it 'interesting to dwellers in Suffolk and Essex' and published in the *Ipswich and Colchester Times*, a paper that had a relatively short life. It must have been the latter improved version that was taken up by Jarrold & Sons for wider circulation.

SPRITTIE

A sprit-rigged barge of the kind used in trading between East Anglian ports, particularly Ipswich, and London. It is probably stretching credulity to trace the ancestry of the barge back to the Roman or Romano-British trading vessels excavated by Peter Marsden at Blackfriars and elsewhere on the Thames in the 1960s, but these craft certainly had a family likeness. The sprit, pronounced

The Ipswich barge Spinaway C, *owned by millers Cranfield Brothers, seen taking part in a race on the River Blackwater in 1962. Built by W.H. Orvis & Co at Ipswich in 1899, she was typical of the vessels that carried cargoes coastwise in the last days of commercial sail.*

spreet by those who sailed in the barges, is a diagonal spar supporting the peak of the mainsail, which is not furled in the usual way but brailed up in the manner of an old-fashioned theatre curtain. This rig could be handled by a very small crew with the aid of winches fitted to the mastcase and elsewhere.

Sprities traded under sail right up to the 1960s, their ability to operate with a crew of two rendering them still economical when other sailing vessels had long been driven off the seas by steam and motor vessels. The last barge to operate commercially, the mulie *Cambria*, was trading under sail under Captain Bob Roberts until 1970. Sprities may still be seen taking part in races on the Orwell and other rivers each summer.

See Frank Carr, *Sailing Barges* (Terence Dalton, 1990)
☛ *See also Paul, R. & W.; Shipyards*

STAYMAKERS

The making of stays or corsets was for many years a significant local industry carried on in the homes of the people involved. In 1830 Ipswich had at least nine staymakers, six of them women, listed in Pigot's *National Commercial Directory*; by 1845 the number had risen to thirteen, only one of whom was male. By the beginning of the twentieth century there were only two women in the town listed in the directory as corset makers, but there were three firms: the Atlas Corset Co in Lower Orwell Street, Brand & Sons in Tacket Street and William Pretty & Son, whose factory in Tower Ramparts employed hundreds of women. In the 1930s the latter company switched to the production of underwear in artificial silk.
☛ *See also Pretty, William, & Son*

STEELYARDS

Early weighing machines, to weigh waggons and their loads, were set up in the eighteenth century when the turnpike trusts realised that heavy traffic was playing havoc with their road surfaces. The trusts began to levy extra tolls on overweight vehicles. There was one on St Margaret's Green, not unlike the example that survives in New Street, Woodbridge. Another was set up in Clay Lane about 1770 by Isaac Brook, who advertised that it was 'entirely of his own projecting and correcting ... for the more convenient, and much more exact, weighing of Hay, Clover, Straw, Waggons (loaded or empty) that use the Turnpike-Road, or other Things of any Weight'.
☛ *See also Clay Lane*

STEPPLES, THE

The stepping-stones at the east end of Orwell Place, used by pedestrians to cross the Wash.
☛ *See also Wash, The*

STOKE BARRACKS

A maltings on the riverside just below Stoke Bridge was converted into a barracks during the Napoleonic Wars at a time when Ipswich contained a large number of troops held in readiness to repel an expected French invasion. It had a parade yard with a pair of folding gates next the street, according to a description given when the government was selling the property off in 1813. The malting reverted to its original purpose, which it served well into the twentieth century. It has now been converted into flats and offices. One of the former malt kilns for a time housed the London Underground computer centre and a large Underground sign continued to adorn the building after the computer centre had moved elsewhere.
☛ *See also Barracks; St Helen's Barracks*

STOKE BRIDGE

The earliest mention of a bridge across the Orwell linking the town with its suburb of Stoke occurs in the tenth century, but it is not clear whether this was a timber or stone structure – or merely a ford, since the word 'bridge' appears to have had both meanings. A ford there certainly was, some yards below the site of the later bridge. It linked the Saxon roads that were much later named Lower Brook Street and Great Whip Street, and the ford continued in use for heavy vehicles long after the construction of the bridge. Indeed, in 1477 it was ordered that carts should not go over Stoke Bridge,

A print of the stone bridge which collapsed during a flood in 1818, to be replaced by a cast-iron bridge brought by canal and by sea from the Black Country. In the background is Stoke windmill on the summit of the hill, and on extreme right is one end of Stoke tidemill.

'but the Bailiffs shall kepe the same locked'. In 1435 John of Cauldwell offered to make a bridge at Stoke Bridge on condition that those using it should pay pontage; the very wording 'a bridge at Stoke Bridge' suggests that the word 'bridge' was being used for the river crossing rather than for a structure.

It is uncertain whether he actually built a bridge, but in 1495 the town authorities ordered that 'All carts going over Stoke bridge lately built, shall pay towards the repayring and maintaining of the same ... provided that none shall goe over the bridge when they may goe through the ffoord'. In 1594, orders were given for timber to be felled on land belonging to the town 'for repairing of bridges broken downe' and for making a rate for the repair of Stoke Bridge and Handford Bridge, and the following year town lands in Bramford were let to two people on terms that included the carting of a number of loads of timber from Whitton and Holbrook for the building of Stoke Bridge. It is fairly certain that these replacement bridges were all of timber construction, and so was the one built in 1669, when a rate was authorised to raise £220.

Joseph Fison's Eastern Union Mills provides a backdrop to this photograph of the southern approach to Stoke Bridge before the replacement of the cast-iron bridge of 1819 by a concrete structure in the 1920s.

A stone bridge did eventually take the place of the last timber one, but that stone bridge was washed away by a flood in April 1818; three men were standing on the bridge 'contemplating the swell and fury of the stream' when two of the three arches suddenly collapsed into the river. The three men went down with the bridge; two were hauled from the river by bystanders but the third was swept away and drowned.

The local authority lost no time in asking William Cubitt, a civil engineer connected with Ransomes, to prepare estimates for reconstruction and for throwing a temporary floating bridge across the river to restore communications. Cubitt estimated that an iron bridge with an arch of 60ft span would cost £3,850, one of brick £3,500. A decision was taken that same day that in spite of the extra cost the bridge should be of cast iron and without further ado the Town Clerk, S. Jackaman, sent an advertisement to the local papers inviting tenders. The contract was awarded to Ransome & Sons, who had already erected at least three cast-iron bridges, but they were not to produce the parts for this big arch themselves. The order for the ironwork went to a firm in Dudley, Worcestershire, from where the bridge sections were sent by canal to Gainsborough on the Trent and then to Ipswich by sea. The new bridge was opened on 19 June 1819, the temporary pontoon bridge was dismantled, and for over a hundred years the cast-iron bridge was a familiar part of the town scene.

It was replaced in the 1920s by a concrete bridge more suitable for modern traffic. When the flow of traffic became too much for the one bridge, a second one was built alongside it in 1982–3.

☛ *See also Ransome & Co.*

STOKE MILLS

The earliest reference to Stoke Mills, or the New Mills as they were often known, is in the mid-fourteenth century when Gilbert de Boulge, William Gunnyld, Henry Walle and John Arnold were granted land to build two watermills; the agreement made with the town was that after this quartet of entrepreneurs had recouped their costs from the income, the mills were to become town property. Richard II seized the mills because the handover of land and the building of the mills had been carried out without royal licence. When Henry IV usurped the throne in 1399 he restored the mills to the town, which had already acquired them before their seizure by the king. Thereafter there appear almost annual references in the town records to the leasing of the New Mills.

To begin with the two waterwheels were turned by the current of the Gipping, but in their later history Stoke Mills harnessed also the water of the tides. Tidal water was admitted to the millpond through sluices on the flood, was penned up there and, as the tide ebbed, was let past the twin wheels to power the mills.

On 15 September 1800, at a time when food prices had risen sharply and there was great distress among the poorer inhabitants of the town, a mob attacked 'Mr. Rainbird's mill' and threatened to burn it down. The Town Clerk read the Riot Act, a brick thrown at his head almost bringing the reading to a premature end, and the Volunteers and then a troop of cavalry from the Barracks were called out to restore order. 'The military, who behaved with praiseworthy moderation, soon dispersed the crowd, after compelling some of the more obstinate to take refuge in the river ... '

The wooden structure of the mill was moved by hydraulic power on 1 September 1877 to the other side of the road. It later became a part of Joseph Fison's Eastern Union Mills that stood on the north bank just above Stoke Bridge, surviving into the early 1930s. Eastern Union Mills became a yeast factory, and was demolished in the late twentieth century.

☛ *See also Handford Mill; Horswade Mill*

STOWMARKET NAVIGATION

Fearing that its own trade would suffer if it allowed cargoes to be carried upriver, Ipswich Corporation resisted proposals in 1719 to make the Gipping navigable to Stowmarket, but in 1790 an Act 'for making and maintaining a navigable Communication between Stowmarket and Ipswich, in the County of Suffolk' received the Royal Assent. Construction of the navigation met with many difficulties, partly through defects in the original survey, and it was not until the autumn of 1793 that it was opened to traffic. There were fifteen locks, almost one for every mile between Ipswich and Stowmarket, but traffic boomed in the early nineteenth century and the effect of the navigation on the economies of Stowmarket and Needham Market was highly beneficial; that of Stowmarket was boosted to the extent that what had been a quiet market town became an industrial centre of some significance. The opening of the wet dock at Ipswich was seen by the proprietors of the barges as a major impediment to their trade, but it was the coming of the railway in 1846 that led to a decline of three-quarters in the tonnage of goods carried on the navigation. Traffic to Stowmarket had declined almost to nothing by the opening of the twentieth century, and the carriage of raw materials to the fertiliser works at Bramford came to an end about 1930. At the last meeting of the trustees in 1934 it was revealed that just £216 remained in the navigation company's account, and this was divided between East Suffolk County Council and the East Suffolk Rivers Catchment Board.

See Edward Paget-Tomlinson, *The Illustrated History of Canal & River Navigations* (Sheffield Academic Press, 1993)

☛ *See also Gipping, River; Orwell, River*

SUFFOLK SHOW

The East Suffolk Agricultural Association was founded in 1831 by a group of forward-looking landowners and farmers, and the first show was held at Wickham Market the following year. West Suffolk began holding its own show in 1833 and until 1856 – when the two associations amalgamated to form the Suffolk Agricultural Association – the two shows ran side by side on the two sides of the county. The show came to Ipswich in 1850 and was held in the town on thirty more occasions between 1853 and 1958; since 1960 it has been held on a permanent showground on Nacton Heath, just east of Ipswich between Bucklesham Road and Felixstowe Road.

TEMPERANCE HALL

Drunkenness was a serious problem in the nineteenth century as working men sought to escape from their thoroughly uncomfortable, indeed comfortless, way of life by resorting to the alehouse. There were those who saw total abstinence as the only answer. Perhaps surprisingly, the temperance movement in Ipswich was inaugurated in 1835 by three soldiers from the Ipswich Barracks, one of whom, Trooper George Greig, called on his hearers to sign the pledge of total abstinence forthwith. The Temperance Hall on the corner of Crown Street and High Street was built in 1840 at the expense of the Quaker banker Richard Dykes Alexander. By 1890 the hall had ceased to have a link with the temperance movement and had become the Crown Street Iron Works where George Abbott made the 'Victoria' cooking ranges that won him gold medals at the 1895 and 1897 Ipswich General Trades and Industrial Exhibitions.
☛ *See also Alexander, Richard Dykes*

THINGSTEAD, THE

St Margaret's Plain was formerly known as the Thingstead, an Anglo-Saxon term for a meeting place. It has been generally assumed that this was the meeting place for the half-hundred of Ipswich, but it may be significant that the Thingstead is outside the town rampart and that, when Ipswich obtained its Charter in 1200, the townsfolk made the churchyard of St Mary-le-Tower their meeting place. Possibly the Thingstead was the meeting place for the five and a half hundreds of the Wicklaw, which was under the jurisdiction of Ely Abbey and was otherwise known as the Liberty of St Etheldreda.

THRASHING MACHINES

The machines produced by Ransomes at Ipswich were always described as thrashers, not threshing machines.
☛ *See also Ransomes, Sims & Jefferies*

THURSBY'S LANE

A very short lane running between Friars Street and Princes Street to the west of Coyte's Gardens, Thursby's Lane disappeared about 1970 when Friars Street was diverted for the erection of the Willis Corroon building. The construction of Princes Street cut the original Thursby's Lane in two, since it originally ran from Friars Street to Elm Street, as can be seen on Pennington's map. In 1856 when the lane was extended to meet the then-new Museum Street, the latter name was applied to the entire length between Westgate Street and Princes Street.

☛ *See also Museum Street; Princes Street*

TOOLEY, HENRY

Little is known of the early years of Henry Tooley, who became one of the most prosperous merchants in Ipswich when the town was enjoying a lucrative trade not only with nearby continental ports but also with Gascony and the Spanish Biscayan ports. It seems likely that he hailed from Catton, a village to the north of Norwich, and that he came to Ipswich during the last quarter of the fifteenth century. By about 1520 he was established as one of the most active merchants in the port, with a factor representing him in the Biscayan ports. About that time he married Alice Purpet, a member of a Suffolk family that seems to have been of some standing in Ipswich. Besides

The new almshouses built for the Tooley's and Smart's foundation in the 1840s. They must have been a great improvement on the original houses built for ten old soldiers.

trading with France and Spain Tooley sent his ship the *Mary Walsingham* 'by the Grace of God Icelandward', whence she returned with stockfish, wind-dried cod. By the time of his death in 1551 Tooley had amassed a considerable fortune, which by his will he left very largely to the setting-up of an almshouse in Ipswich for ten persons who 'shall be tryed unfaynedlye lame by occasyon of the kynges warres or otherwise that cannot acquire and gette their livinge or the oone half thereof'. Tooley's foundation was later joined with that of William Smart, and the nineteenth-century successors to his almshouses are still performing a useful service in the town.

See John Webb, *Great Tooley of Ipswich* (Suffolk Records Society 1962)

TORCS, THE IPSWICH

A sandy bank was being levelled for new houses at Belstead Hills in 1968 when the bulldozer driver noticed several objects in the soil pushed up by his machine. The objects turned out to be five Iron-Age gold torcs, necklets worn perhaps by tribal leaders as a mark of their authority. It is possible they formed part of a goldsmith's stock, buried for safekeeping when danger threatened, or they may have been deposited beside the holy well mentioned in the Anglo-Saxon bounds of Stoke in the tenth century. Although experts from Ipswich Museum were called in to investigate, no trace of a burial or of anything else of significance was found on the site. Two years later the owner of one of the new houses found a sixth torc just inches below the surface of his garden; it seems that it was in soil that had been spread widely before the bulldozer driver found the other five. These outstanding examples of ancient craftsmanship are now in the British Museum, while replicas are to be seen in Ipswich Museum.

☛ *See also Holy Wells*

TOWER RAMPARTS

Now an open space used as a station for the town's buses, this name originally applied to that section of the town bank within the parish of St Mary-le-Tower; earlier, the roadway in the ditch inside the rampart had been Tower Ditches. Until the 1930s there were houses perched on the bank, facing Tower Ramparts and with

Houses built on the town bank in Tower Ramparts in the 1930s. The houses were demolished and the historic rampart levelled when Tower Ramparts became first a car park and then a bus station.

their backs to Crown Street; photographs show the houses approached by steps up the face of the bank. Similar houses and steps existed in St Margaret's Ditches, later Old Foundry Road.

TOWN HALL

The present Town Hall was built in 1866–7 to a design by a Lincoln architect, Pearson Bellamy, who rather specialised in town halls. The work of erecting it was entrusted to Ipswich builder Edward Gibbons, whose tender of £11,749 was the lowest of five received. With its building, the last remnants of the old St Mildred's Church were cleared away after about a thousand years. The new building was opened in the last week of January 1868, the Mayor, John Patteson Cobbold, inviting 'above 600 of the principal citizens' to a 'Conversazione' in the Council Chamber on the Monday evening, when 'much was done to make the immense multitude of guests comfortable'. Exactly how they were all fitted in is not recorded.

The building seems to have had its teething troubles: there were complaints about the ventilation of the Sessions Court and about the heating of the Council Chamber, and protests from members of the council about the poor acoustics of the latter room. Then came tragedy. In 1879 a heavy piece of stone fell from under the upper cornice of the Town Hall and killed a young man named Robert Davey who was on his way to work. It was found that the Bath stone had absorbed rainwater, which had then frozen and cracked the stone. The necessary repairs cost more than £3,000, and the corporation paid Robert's father £5 to provide a headstone and footstone for his grave.

For a hundred years the Town Hall was the centre of local government, but there came a time when, in spite of numerous partitions dividing it into more and more small offices, it was simply not large enough to accommodate all the council departments. In the 1960s a lofty tower block known as the Civic Centre was built between Black Horse Lane and the new Civic Drive to house the various borough council departments. The Town Hall was refurbished for community uses at the same time that the Corn Exchange was converted into an entertainment and arts centre, but the Council Chamber is still the meeting place of the borough council.

See R.L. Cross, *The Living Past – A Victorian Heritage* (Borough of Ipswich, 1975)

☛ *See also Cornhill; St Mildred's Church*

TOWN LIBRARY

When he died in 1599 William Smarte, a rich Ipswich draper, left 'my latten printed bookes and writen bookes in volume and p'chmente ... towards one librarye safelie to be keepte in the vestrye of the parishe church of St Mary

Tower', thus providing the basis of the Town Library. For some time the books remained in an old chest, but about 1610 Samuel Ward, the Town Preacher, was given the task of preparing a room in the former Blackfriars for housing a library to which further benefactors gave books. The library remained there until in 1832 it was put in the care of the Ipswich Literary Institution formed that year; it is now housed at Ipswich School in the care of the headmaster.

See John Blatchly, *The Town Library of Ipswich Provided for the Use of the Town Preachers in 1599: A history and catalogue* (Boydell Press 1989)
☛ *See also Beck, Cave*

TRAMS, ELECTRIC

Ipswich Corporation obtained powers to establish an electricity undertaking in 1897, and the Ipswich Corporation Tramways Act of 1900 authorised the laying of an electric tramway in the town. The horse trams, compulsorily acquired by the corporation in 1901, ceased running on 6 June 1903 and the electric trams entered public service a little more than five months later on a route from Whitton to Cornhill, the railway station and Bourne Bridge, with a spur along Bath Street to connect with the GER river steamers. Other routes to Lattice Barn and Derby Road station, along Bramford Road, down Queen Street to Stoke Bridge and on to Bourne Bridge, and to the Royal Oak at the

Tramcar No 2 making its way along Princes Street towards the railway station passes the Friars Street junction.

junction of Felixstowe Road and Derby Road were all operating by Whitsun 1904. There were thirty-six green-and-cream tramcars, double-deckers with open tops; Board of Trade regulations did not allow covered-in double-deckers to run on the 3ft 6in gauge used in Ipswich. The tramcars were stabled in large car sheds built on the corner of Constantine Road and Portman's Walk next door to the electricity generating station, which was equipped with generators driven by high-speed steam engines made in Ipswich by Reavells.

The coming of war in 1914 had a dire effect on the tramway. As drivers and conductors left to join the services women were taken on as conductresses, but were dismissed when the war ended. Maintenance of the track and overhead wires became more and more difficult. Much of the track in Bath Street was lifted for use in replacing worn rails on other parts of the system, but the deteriorating condition of the tramlines caused the cars to sway violently, to the concern and discomfort of passengers. The tramway undertaking was responsible for repair of the roadway between the rails, which placed a serious burden on the Tramways Department, just as it had on the Ipswich Tramways Company in the days of the horse trams.

As costs escalated and the system deteriorated, the management decided to try 'trackless trams', trolleybuses on solid-rubber tyres. The experiment proved successful, and in 1926 the trams were all taken to the end of the line in Norwich Road, where the bodies were lifted from the four-wheeled trucks to be sold for use as chicken coops and garden sheds. Ipswich was the first town in the country to change from trams to trolleybuses.

☛ *See also Trams, Horse; Transport Museum, Ipswich; Trolleybuses*

TRAMS, HORSE

The introduction of trams to Ipswich in 1880 was unpopular with an influential section of the population. Such was their opposition that the trams were not allowed to run through the town centre; and, when the first tram, pulled by a single horse, was derailed as it carried the Mayor and Town Clerk on a trial trip, the cabbies were overjoyed. Nevertheless, the tramway opened to the public on 13 October 1880 (no, it was not a Friday!), but it was six months before a second route was opened from Princes Street along Portman Road to Norwich Road. The Ipswich Tramways Company was incorporated by Act of Parliament in 1881 and the original promoter sold his shares to the company. This Act authorised a route from Barrack Corner as far as the Cornhill to link with that along Princes Street, and in the summer of 1883 a further route was opened from Majors Corner to Derby Road station, an extra horse having to be attached to the trams to get them up the St John's Road hill. There was still no link between Majors Corner and the Cornhill. That gap was not closed until June 1884, and then a tradesman made a last stand by leaving his pony and trap on the tramlines in Carr Street; he held up the trams for almost half an hour.

The horse tram depot in Quadling Street in its last days, with the bulk of the Greyfriars complex looming behind it. The tram rails can be seen in the yard running into the wooden tram shed.

The car shed and stables were in Quadling Street, on the corner of Cecilia Street; while the Majors Corner to Derby Road section was isolated, there was also a car shed beside the Railway Hotel in Foxhall Road.

The service closed for a couple of weeks in 1893 when the wood paving between the rails was replaced by the corporation, which sent the bill to the tramway company; it was unable to pay, and the trams stopped running. However, agreement was reached and the trams resumed service after two weeks. The tramway company never did pay its shareholders a dividend. The corporation compulsorily acquired the horse tramway in 1901 and set about replacing it with an electric tramway. The horse trams ceased running in June 1903 and the rails were lifted, being too light for the electric trams; the nine trams were sold, to become chicken sheds and the like, and the twenty-seven horses were auctioned off to new owners.

See Robert Markham, *Public Transport in Ipswich 1880–1970* (Ipswich Information Office, 1970)

☛ *See also Trams, Electric; Transport Museum, Ipswich; Trolleybuses*

TRANSPORT MUSEUM, IPSWICH

Founded by a team of enthusiasts in 1965 as the Ipswich Transport Preservation Group, the Ipswich Transport Museum has the largest collection of transport items in Britain devoted to a single town. Every one of more than a hundred vehicles and examples of local engineering in the museum was either made or used in and around the town. Since 1988 the collection has been housed in the former trolleybus depot at Priory Heath, on the eastern outskirts of the town; until then the collection had been hidden away in temporary storage, some vehicles in barns and sheds and some in the open. Frequent moves from one place to another, coupled with exposure to the elements and the attacks of vandals, took their toll on the exhibits, but thanks to the work of a dedicated team of volunteers the collection has survived and many of the vehicles, including an electric tram dating from the beginning of the twentieth century, are now being restored to their original condition. Operated entirely by unpaid volunteers, the museum is open to the public regularly throughout the summer, with special events such as 'Wheels by Lamplight' and the Ipswich to Felixstowe Run throughout the year; support is given by the Friends of the Ipswich Transport Museum, who hold monthly meetings during the winter months. The museum possesses an impressive set of Ipswich buses, most of which are in running order and are from time to time seen on the road; a popular annual event is a 'bus operating day' when visitors can ride on the vehicles.

TROLLEYBUSES

Ipswich was the first town in Britain to abandon trams in favour of trolleybuses, vehicles taking current from overhead wires but running on ordinary road wheels rather than on tracks. During the First World War there was heavy wear on the tram tracks and little maintenance was possible, and by 1922 some streets in the town centre were needing repair. The Tramways Department of the corporation was responsible for much of the cost, and it could not find the necessary money from the tramway operation. The decision was made to experiment with 'trackless trams' on the route from the Cornhill to the railway station and three vehicles were hired from Railless Ltd of Rochester; the vehicles were equipped for one-man operation, the driver acting also as conductor, a fairly revolutionary concept at the time.

The trolleybuses proved a success, the three vehicles were bought from Railless and a fourth trolleybus – made in Ipswich by Ransomes, Sims & Jefferies – was purchased in 1924. An Act of Parliament the following year allowed the corporation to replace all the trams by trolleybuses, and in 1926 thirty more trolleybuses entered service, half of them built by Ransomes and half by Richard Garrett of Leiston.

All the early trolleybuses were single-deckers, but in 1933 double-deck vehicles built by Ransomes were introduced, more being built the following year when the London Road route was extended to serve the Royal Show of that year. Ransomes also built trolleybuses for other towns, including Nottingham, Maidstone and St Helens, and for export to Europe, South Africa, Singapore and other parts of the world. During the Second World

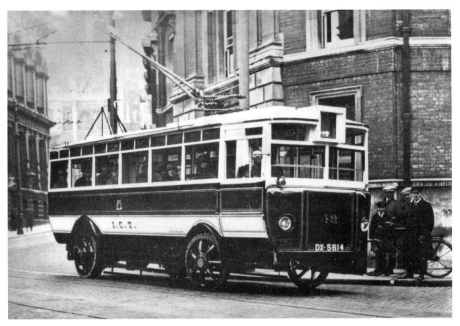

One of the first Ipswich Corporation Transport trolleybuses or 'trackless trams' heading down Queen Street from the Cornhill; note the solid rubber tyres, later replaced by pneumatic tyres.

War women took over not only as 'clippies' but as trolleybus drivers. The first motor buses were introduced in 1950, and the last trolleybus ran in the town on 23 August 1963.

Some of the Ipswich trolleybuses were sold to Walsall Corporation for further use and one of these, no. 126 (Walsall no. 347), was acquired for preservation by local enthusiasts; it is now to be seen in the Ipswich Transport Museum in the former Priory Heath trolleybus depot, which was opened originally in 1937.

☛ *See also Trams, Electric; Trams, Horse; Transport Museum, Ipswich*

TURNER, E.R. & F.

One of the first tasks undertaken by the firm of Bond, Turner & Hurwood when it was established in 1837 at St Peter's Iron Works, between College Street and the river, was the construction of the lock gates for the Wet Dock. In later years this small ironfounding and general engineering business was to develop into a firm of milling engineers, who were among the pioneers of roller milling. When George Hurwood left the partnership to become engineer to the Ipswich Dock Commissioners, the business was carried on first by Walton Turner and then by his sons Edward Rush Turner and Frederick Turner, eventually becoming E.R. & F. Turner, by which name it became nationally and internationally known. In 1849 they acquired a second works in the town, Greyfriars Works, which stood where Cardinal Park has now been developed, and began the manufacture of steam engines, many designed especially for use in mills. The firm increasingly specialised in milling machinery and many complete milling plants, including steam engines to drive them, were made for erection in Britain or abroad. The firm gave up building steam engines at the beginning of the twentieth century, when the decision was taken to concentrate on flour-milling and mining machinery, and equipment for gold mines, the latter exported to South Africa. As early as 1863 Turners were manufacturing roller mills for use in conjunction with stone mills for the gradual reduction of wheat to flour, and during the 1880s the firm was one of a number of British companies to introduce the complete roller-milling system into England from Hungary.

In the 1920s Turners began making electric motors for various purposes: among other things they powered trolleybuses built by Ransomes, Sims & Jefferies and mobile cranes produced by Ransomes & Rapier. Turners survived the collapse of Agricultural and General Engineers Ltd, of which they had become a part in 1919, and continued manufacture of milling machinery and electric motors, moving part of their production to a new works on the site of the former Valley Brickworks in Foxhall Road in the 1930s. Bull Motors continued to operate on the Foxhall Road site into quite recent years, but the milling side of the business was taken over by another milling engineer some time after the Second World War.

☞ *See also Bull Motors*

UMBRELLA, THE

With the opening of the Wet Dock in the 1840s, a fine Promenade with an avenue of lime trees was laid out alongside the New Cut. At one end of this popular amenity was a shelter with an ogee-shaped roof that was always known as The Umbrella. The Promenade fell victim to dock expansion between the First and Second World Wars, but The Umbrella remained into the 1950s.

☞ *See also Promenade, The; Wet Dock*

UNITARIAN MEETING HOUSE

One of the finest early Nonconformist churches in the country, what is now known as the Unitarian Meeting House was built in 1699–1700 as the Presbyterian Meeting House on a site in Boat Lane (now Friars Street) bought by Thomas Bantoft, mercer, for £150. Following purchase of the site, a contract was drawn up and signed by six members of the congregation and by Joseph Clark, house carpenter. From the contract, still in the possession of the congregation, we learn that the building was to cost £257, excluding glazing of the windows, the galleries, pews and pulpit. Of this sum £10 was paid to Clark in advance. In the contract, Clark agreed:

> That he the said Joseph Clark his servants and assigns shall and will at his own proper costs and charges take downe All those outhouses and old Tymber-wall designed to be taken downe standing on the West side in the Yard belonging to the Capitall Messuage which the said Thomas Bantoft hath lately purchased of Mr. Thomas Bloss situate, lyeing and being in the parish of St Nicholas in Ipswich aforesaid and that he the said Joseph Clark his Executors and Assigns shall and will at his and their proper costs and charges in good orderly and workmanlike manner make and newe build to and for the uses of them ... in the aforesaid yard and upon the ground where the said Outhouses are to be taken downe A good new strong and substanciall house for a meeting-place which shalbe in length sixtie foot and in Breadthe fiftie foot, To be built with a double Roofe and to have four Lucums [dormer windows] in the Roofe thereof fronting to the North, The Roofe of which said building to be boorne up in the middle with four good and substanciall Cullums [columns].

An old photograph by William Vick of the Unitarian Meeting House, built in 1700 at a time when the Dissenters were enjoying a new-found freedom of worship.

Besides paying the cost of the work in instalments the six men agreed to:

> provide and give unto the said Joseph Clark and his servants four Barrels
> of good small Beere for to drink whilst imployed in the said Building.

That provision was doubtless intended to ensure that they did not waste time
adjourning to a nearby hostelry to quench their thirsts. The galleries were not
mentioned in the contract; they cost another £96, which was paid in
instalments. Another additional item was the handsome pulpit, with its
magnificent carving in the style of Grinling Gibbons; it is generally assumed
to have been the product of one of the great carver's pupils.

The trust deed drawn up by the minister and the leading members of the
congregation in 1710 did not lay down any doctrine, and in the course of the
eighteenth century the congregation gradually moved away from the doctrine
of the Trinity and by the end of that century was avowedly Unitarian. Since
that time this timber-framed meeting house has been known as the Unitarian
Meeting House.

See Cliff Reed, *A Suffolk Tabernacle: The Ipswich Unitarian Meeting House*
(Ipswich, 1998)

VERNON STREET

The old way from Stoke Bridge to Wherstead Road was up the narrow Bell
Lane into Austin Street, or else left into Dock Lane and right into Great
Whip Street. In the mid-nineteenth century a new road, named after Admiral
Vernon of Orwell Park, was cut through direct from Stoke Bridge to the
junction of Austin Street, Great Whip Street and Wherstead Road.
☛ *See also Bell, The Old; Stoke Bridge*

VICK, WILLIAM

Two volumes of photographic views of Ipswich in the nineteenth century
produced by William Vick provide a fascinating glimpse of the town as it once
was, but only the keenest collector can afford to acquire them today. Vick
took over the business of William Cobb, 'photographic artist', about 1870
and also took over Cobb's negatives, which included views of the town in
mid-century. These proved useful when Vick began to trade on the wave of
nostalgia for the pre-Victorian town that swept across the better-off sections
of the community as old buildings that had survived from the Middle Ages
were demolished and replaced by fine Victorian shops. So popular were some
views of the town that Vick had difficulty in printing enough copies from a
single negative, and among the glass plates now in the Suffolk Record Office
are positive plates that were used to make multiple copy negatives; these were
employed to produce daylight prints in his studio at Barrack Corner, on the

junction of Clarkson Street and London Road. One of his prints, captioned 'Old Butter Market and Queen Street, 1830', was probably taken by his predecessor, but not in 1830; the first negatives did not appear until the 1840s. Like Cobb, William Vick described himself both as photographer and artist, and on the reverse of his photo mounts he offered 'Enlargements finished in oil, water-colours or monochrome'. A member of the Ipswich Scientific Society, founded in 1869 'to excite interest in the study of biology, botany, chemistry, natural science in general, and archaeology', Vick gave the members the benefit of his photographic experience 'in a well-compiled paper'. He also took his camera on some of the society's 'field days' and on excursions such as that taken by a group of members to the Broads. He retired about 1899 and went to live in Raynes Park, dying there in 1911 at the age of 77. His glass negatives were bought and deposited in the Ipswich Museum, thus preserving an extraordinary record of the nineteenth-century town; they have since been transferred to the Suffolk Record Office.

WALLS, TOWN

The town was first surrounded by a defensive ditch and bank during the Danish occupation, perhaps in response to the advance of the army of Wessex early in the tenth century; the ditch was filled in and then redug some time in the following century, possibly as a defence against the Vikings who 'harried' the town in 991 and again landed at Ipswich in 1010. The town rampart and ditch were reconstructed in 1203, three years after the town had gained its Charter from King John, and a grant of murage was obtained from King Edward I in 1299 which entitled the authorities to raise money for repairing the defences. In 1302 'a parcell of the Town Ditches

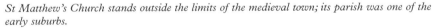

St Matthew's Church stands outside the limits of the medieval town; its parish was one of the early suburbs.

[was] granted to Robert Joyliffe, at the yearly rent of sixpence for ever, unless it comes to pass that the town shall be enclosed with a stone wall', and then in 1352 the town obtained a licence to strengthen the town with a stone wall, but it would seem this was never built. An order made in 1604 that a gravelled path should be laid along the top of the 'walls' makes it obvious that the reference is to an earthen bank and not a stone wall. At the time of the Civil Wars the 'walls' were put in order and the staunchly Puritan town authorities ordered crossing places to be stopped up in case of an attack by Royalist forces. Nevertheless, the rampart and its ditch continued to mark out the town until the nineteenth century at least, though there were extra-mural suburbs such as St Helen's, St Clement's and St Matthew's from a much earlier period.

☞ *See also Bull Gate; East Gate; North Gate; West Gate*

WALTERS, HARRY

One of the town's best-known photographers at the beginning of the twentieth century, Harry Walters made his first camera for himself using bits and pieces such as a cardboard pillbox which served as a lens holder. As a professional photographer he had premises next door to the Running Buck on St Margaret's Plain; over the door was a large sign bearing the words 'Secure the Shadow ere the Substance fade'. In an age of largely homespun entertainment, Walters – or Harry Wilmott as he called himself when appearing on the stage – took part in popular concerts at the Co-operative Hall and other local venues. With a number of friends he formed a group known as the Snowflake Minstrels, which was well known in the town and the surrounding area. A man with a great sense of fun, he revelled in trick photography: when Queen Victoria's statue was being erected in front of Christchurch Mansion, a stone's throw from his studio, he contrived to take a photograph of himself dressed as a minstrel standing in front of it on the plinth and issued it as a postcard with the caption 'Harry Wilmott, negro comedian'. He used to show it to people with the comment 'That's Harry Wilmott as he appeared before the Queen'. He continued to run his photographic business up to the time of his death in 1926.

WARD, SAMUEL

The most notable of a line of Town Lecturers, Samuel Ward was about 28 when he was appointed by the corporation in 1605. A staunch Puritan, he found himself from time to time in conflict with the Bishop of Norwich and with the king, but his uncompromising adherence to Puritan principles found favour with the town authorities. In spite of terms of imprisonment, he remained in his post right up to his death in 1640. He had in fact been elected Town Lecturer for life in 1607, 'if he shall soe long dwell in this Towne'.

A tract for which he drew the title-page design, showing the pope, the cardinals and the king of Spain in conference with the Devil, brought him into collision with the king in 1621. James was at that time negotiating with Spain to arrange a marriage between his son Charles and the Infanta Maria, and Ward's depiction of the Armada being dispersed by storms sent by divine intervention and of Guy Fawkes approaching the Houses of Parliament, watched by the Eye of God, might have been entirely patriotic but was at that moment politically incorrect. When the Spanish ambassador complained, Ward was committed to prison, from which he was eventually released after pleading that he had had no sinister intention of meddling in any of his majesty's 'secrett affaires'.

That was not Ward's only experience of imprisonment. In 1635 he was suspended from preaching and committed to prison after being accused of having 'preached against the common bowing at the name of Jesus, and against the king's *Book of Sports*, and further said that the Church of England was ready to ring changes in religion, and the gospel stood on tiptoe, as ready to be gone'. In this and other predicaments the Corporation of Ipswich stood by its Town Lecturer; Matthew Wren, who became Bishop of Norwich in 1635, reported to Archbishop Laud with some feeling that Ipswich was proving to be the 'most refractory and styf place' in his whole diocese.

When Samuel Ward died in March 1640, the corporation granted his widow and eldest son a generous pension of £100 a year.

WASH, THE

What is now Upper and Lower Orwell Street used to be known, and to older people still is known, as the Wash, a folk memory of the days when a stream flowed from the Cauldwell Hall estate down what is now Spring Road and ran through these streets on its way into the Orwell. At the junction with Orwell Place and Eagle Street were the Stepples, stepping-stones that enabled walkers to negotiate the stream and the surrounding muddy ground; Orwell Place was formerly known as Stepples Street, and is so shown on Pennington's map. Some of the old stepples were discovered when the roadway was being repaired in 1886. While the name of the Wash might be taken to indicate no more than a place washed by the stream, it did have another meaning: the washing of clothes, prohibited at the conduit in Tavern Street, was permitted at the Common Wash, a particular part of the Wash.
☛ *See also Stepples, The*

WEST GATE

The main entrance to the town from north and west, the West or St Matthew's Bar Gate stood just to the west of Black Horse Lane. A very substantial building of stone and brick, it had quite a large arch with a headroom of about 15ft (4.5m) to admit carts and waggons as well as people on foot and horseback, but when the gates were shut, locked and barred it would have proved an impregnable obstacle to unwelcome visitors. Pictures show it to have been sturdily built, giving an impression of solidity and strength. On the outside the gate was flanked by two projecting towers. The date of its original building is unknown, but it would have been some time in the fourteenth century, soon after the construction of the 'walls' which consisted of an earthen rampart and a ditch. The stone lower storey was possibly part of the original gate, and it is likely that the brick upper storey was part of the rebuilding of the gate in 1448 by John de Caldwell.

From that time onwards the gate served as the borough gaol, though in the eighteenth century this was transferred to two houses on the east side of Black Horse Lane, or Old Gaol Lane as it was once known. In 1556, during the reign of Queen Mary, the 'keeper of the gaol' was Richard Bird, a Protestant who seems to have had much sympathy with some of those incarcerated for their religious beliefs. In a document of 18 May 1556 he was accused of having 'by evil counsel animated the prisoners of his sect'; it was also complained that he and his wife 'did cheek the Commissioners with unseemly words, tending almost to a tumult'. He told 'em!

The West Gate proved such an obstruction to traffic by the eighteenth century that it was demolished in 1781. It had stood at the end of Westgate Street for some four hundred years.

After ceasing to be a prison the upper rooms in the gate were used by the army as a gunpowder magazine and a lower room as a guardroom, but this came to an end in 1780 when local people, worried about the risk of an explosion in the not unlikely event of a fire, successfully petitioned for the gunpowder to be stored somewhere else. The following year it was decided at a Great Court 'That St Matthew's Gate in this town and borough be sold to the best bidder in order that the same may be pulled down'. And sold it was, for £32, to somebody who doubtless made a considerable profit out of the building materials recovered during the demolition.

☛ *See also Bull Gate; East Gate; North Gate; Walls, Town*

WESTGATE STREET

Leading west from the Cornhill, Westgate Street took its name from the West Gate of the town which stood near the junction of Westgate and Crown Street. At the time Ogilby surveyed his map in 1674, the gate was in use as the borough gaol; some of the early Quakers were held prisoner there. The western part of the street was then known as Gaol Gate Street, the section nearest the Cornhill being named Bargate Street.

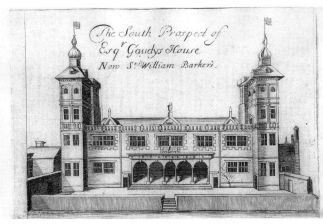

Thomas Seckford's Great Place in Westgate Street, seen from the south side in the seventeenth century. Much of this fine old building was lost when Museum Street was built in the 1840s.

☛ *See also West Gate; Clay Lane; Cornhill*

WET DOCK

When it was opened one dull February day in 1842 the Wet Dock, with a total water area of 33 acres, was the largest enclosed dock in the country, apart from the Floating Harbour at Bristol. Its construction, which took four years and cost over £100,000, paved the way for the commercial and industrial success of the town in the Victorian period. Designed by a leading London engineer, Henry Palmer, and built under his supervision, the dock was formed by building embankments at both ends of a broad bend of the Orwell, digging a cut-off channel to carry the water of the Gipping, and constructing a lock to admit ships to the dock without letting the water out of the dock at low tide. Ships would no longer have to sit on the mud at low

Sailing barges entering the Dock through the new lock, opened in 1881. The recess in the lock wall on the left was provided for a swing bridge, though this was not constructed until more than twenty years later.

tide, with all the dangers of straining a vessel on a bad berth, but would be able to float alongside the quays at all states of the tide.

It is likely that Palmer was aware of the earlier plans of William Chapman, who in several reports had advocated the construction of a dock with the excavation of a New Cut to carry the river flow. Besides the dock itself Palmer designed the timber-framed dockside warehouses, which extended right across the new quay that was to run along the north and east sides of the dock. Previously, much of the waterfront had no quayside: buildings came right down to the river. As work progressed on the dock, Palmer found himself in conflict with some of the Dock Commissioners and with the contractor, David Thornbory, who saw no reason either to obey the engineer's directions or to work to the specifications he had been given. Thornbory seems to have gained the upper hand over the unfortunate engineer by getting himself elected a Dock Commissioner.

The foundation stone of the entrance lock was laid on 26 June 1839 by the Mayor, George Green Sampson, watched by some 15,000 people, if contemporary reports are to be believed. The bandsmen of the 9th Lancers, their tunics faced with scarlet and blue, were there to entertain the crowd as they awaited the appearance of the civic procession and cannons boomed out as the Mayor and Corporation, accompanied by a bodyguard of Borough Police, made their way through a triumphal arch bearing the motto 'May Ipswich Flourish'. More than two and a half years went by before the lock gates could be closed to keep out the tide and hold the water in the dock, and the opening ceremony seems to have been a low-key affair.

Darkness was already closing in on 17 January 1842 when John Chevallier Cobbold, Mayor and Dock Commissioner, boarded the little sloop *Director* as she headed out of the lock on the way to Rochester with a cargo of grain and goods; presumably he stepped ashore, perhaps somewhere near the family brewery at the Cliff, before she headed downriver on her voyage. There was scant ceremony and the *Ipswich Journal*, a Tory local newspaper that had opposed the dock plans from the beginning, sought to damn the whole proceedings with faint praise: 'Thus, after no inconsiderable bungling and delay, the town may be said to enjoy the advantages of a Wet Dock'.

In spite of the castigation of the *Ipswich Journal*, the Wet Dock allowed Ipswich to enjoy the enhanced trade of the Victorian age. By the second decade of the twentieth century, expansion outside the dock was necessary to cope with bigger ships and the volume of trade, but the dock continued to be well used until the development of the West Bank terminal along the Wherstead Road in the 1970s. In 2004 the dock was largely occupied by a yacht marina, with expensive residential development replacing the old commercial dockside buildings.

See Bob Malster & Bob Jones, *A Victorian Vision, The Building of Ipswich Wet Dock* (Ipswich Port Authority, 1992)

☞ *See also Chapman, Williams; Dock Commissioners;* **Ipswich Journal;** *Palmer, Henry; River Commissioners*

Shipping in the Wet Dock about 1970; today the dock is a marina and the site of the ballast depot on the right is now occupied by apartment blocks.

WHALE FISHERY

There appeared in the *Ipswich Journal* of 26 August 1786 an advertisement calling for subscriptions of £100 and upwards for a new venture to be based on the Orwell:

> Several Gentlemen of the Town of Ipswich, having considered the advantages which have arisen in many ports of this kingdom, from a WHALE FISHERY, and being convinced that the port of Ipswich, is most commodiously situated for that purpose, have opened a book at the Banking-House of Messrs. Crickitt, Truelove and Kerridge, for receiving Subscriptions for establishing such a trade here.

Two companies were formed in Ipswich, one promoted by banker Charles Crickitt and the other by banker Emerson Cornwell and shipbuilder Captain Timothy Mangles. In spite of the wording of the advertisement, Crickitt's ships – the *Simond* and the *Charlotte*, the latter chartered from its owner – operated from the Thames, whose facilities for dealing with the products of whaling would undoubtedly have been superior to those of the Orwell. The other company's vessels, the *Ipswich* and the chartered *Orwell*, with crews of between forty and fifty men each, also sailed from the Thames in March 1787 for their first season in northern waters, but both entered the Orwell on their return, and their story can be traced through the news columns of the *Ipswich Journal*.

The *Orwell* had a successful season, taking seven whales, which provided 150 butts of blubber and about 4cwt (200kg) of whalebone, that horny material that filters out the plankton from the seawater ingested by the giant mammals. Though the ship could not get beyond Downham Bridge because of the poor state of the river, the blubber was taken in lighters up to Nova Scotia, on the west bank of the river a little way below the town, where the boilers for rendering down the blubber had been erected, and 'the noisome cookery' began. One might have expected a general exodus from the town on account of the stench of boiling blubber, but the newspaper reported that 'the stench did not reach any part of the town, neither was it scarcely to be smelled within 100 yards of the place'. Believe that if you can! The *Ipswich* caught no whales that season, but she did bring 1½ butts of blubber, the results of the slaughter of fifty-four seals.

The next year Cornwell and Mangles sent out a third ship as well as the *Ipswich* and the *Orwell*, but both they and Crickitt's ships had a poor season. Nor was the 1789 season successful, with the result that Cornwell and Mangles abandoned the whaling trade. Crickitt continued to send out the *Simond* until 1791, but when she returned 'clean' (without any whales) that year he also gave up. The rendering plant at Nova Scotia, the try works as it was called, was put up for sale in 1793, and the whaleboats, harpoons, lances and other equipment from the *Ipswich* and another vessel were advertised early the following year. Although the historian G.R. Clarke commented in 1830 that 'it is probable that another attempt would be more successful' none of the Ipswich shipowners took the risk.

See Hugh Moffat, *Ships and Shipyards of Ipswich 1700–1970* (Malthouse Press, 2002)

☞ *See also Shipyards;* Ipswich Journal*; Orwell, River*

WHERRIES

The wherries that carried passengers and parcels between Ipswich and Harwich and other places on the Orwell were nothing like the wherries of the Broadland rivers; judging from eighteenth-century paintings, the only record we have, they were boats about 20ft (6m) in length, with two masts rigged with fore-and-aft sails. Their busiest period came during the wars with France; it was said in 1793 that the wherries going downriver were so crowded that every day passengers were being left behind, and the historian G.R. Clarke records that as many as twenty or thirty open boats were known to leave Ipswich in a single day with passengers for Harwich. The Cole and Woolward families operated the wherries in the eighteenth century; John Woolward, whose gravestone in St Clement's churchyard describes him as 'master of the wherry', was killed along with three of his passengers when his wherry was struck by lightning in July 1708 while on its way upriver to Ipswich.

☞ *See also Orwell, River*

WHITEFRIARS

The Carmelite friary or Whitefriars, so called from the white habit of the friars, stood to the south of the Buttermarket, where remains of some of the buildings survived into the nineteenth century to be photographed by William Vick. Founded in 1278–9, the friary expanded in the fourteenth century to fill much of the area between the Buttermarket and Falcon Street and between Queen Street and St Stephen's Lane. Completion of rebuilding of the friary church was marked by its consecration in 1477. King Henry VI and his court were entertained at the friary in 1452.

The last remains of the Carmelite friary photographed by William Vick towards the end of the nineteenth century; they have not survived.

WHITE HORSE, GREAT

There has been an inn on the site of the Great White Horse Hotel – at the east end of Tavern Street, on the Northgate Street corner – since at least 1518, but it is highly likely that there had been a hostelry there long before that. The 'Great' in the title indicates the place this inn occupies in the history and affection of the town. The White Horse was the town's premier inn: when George II came to Ipswich in 1736 on his way from Lowestoft to London, it was at the White Horse that he rested and received expressions of loyalty from the bailiffs and members of the corporation. And in 1800 Lord Nelson, accompanied by Sir William and Lady Hamilton, stopped at the Great White Horse, having found Nelson's house, Roundwood, locked and shuttered because Lady Nelson had gone to London to prepare a welcome there for her husband.

In 1818 the Great White Horse lost its timbered front in the interests of widening Tavern Street; G.R. Clarke says in his history of Ipswich, 'The Old White Horse was almost entirely pulled down, and the present handsome and commodious building erected in its stead'. In fact quite a lot of the old building survived behind the new frontage of fashionable Suffolk white bricks. It was probably at this time that the 'rampaging horse' described by Dickens in *Pickwick Papers* was placed over the main entrance in Tavern Street; it is said to have been banished later to that other White Horse at Tattingstone, on the Manningtree road. Though not a coaching inn, the Great White Horse had extensive stables at the rear where a posting service operated, providing horses for onward travel by gentlemen in their own coaches.

In the twentieth century it was still a watering hole favoured by many of the town's prominent citizens, but there came a time when it was threatened with closure; it was stated that the motoring fraternity now demanded hotels on the outskirts rather than in the town centre. After a period when shop fronts were incorporated into the familiar Tavern Street frontage, the hotel returned to its earlier appearance, and at the start of the twenty-first century it still served much the same purpose it had served for at least five hundred years.
☛ *See also Assembly Rooms*

WILLIS CORROON

Willis, Faber & Dumas, as the company was then known, came to Ipswich in the 1970s after making a decision to rationalise its operations and move all its administrative departments from Southend and London to Suffolk. The firm appointed Norman Foster as architect for a new building to be erected on a site between Friars Street, Princes Street and Franciscan Way, his brief being that the office block was to be more than just 'a paper factory'. He was specifically asked for a distinguished building that would be 'neither over ambitious nor pedestrian' and that would provide an office environment

Buildings on the north side of Friars Street are seen in the glass of the Willis Corroon offices.

'sympathetic to human values'. Down came the corner premises of Alfred Clark, old-established saddler and manufacturer of leather goods, the British Lion public house with its Coadestone lion on the parapet, the Friars Head public house and a number of other buildings, and construction of the new offices started in May 1972.

In spite of delivery delays and steel shortages, a period when work was limited to three days a week and other problems the £6.5 million building was completed in February 1975, only one month late. The glass-walled building with its internal swimming pool and roof garden, and with central escalators giving easy access to the upper floors, did not gain immediate acceptance in the town, its radical design attracting criticism from those who found its unadorned expanse of dark glass unappealing.

There were those who foresaw that visiting football fans on their way to Portman Road would wreak havoc on the glass wall. 'What would happen if somebody threw a brick at it?' the architect was asked. Norman Foster arranged a test on a mock-up of the wall, and the brick bounced back from the unbroken glass.

The exterior cladding of Pilkington's toughened 'Antisun' bronze float-glass is hung on a curtain-wall principle, being fixed to the main structure only at roof level. When the 1987 hurricane blew in the glass wall on the Franciscan Way side of the building many thought that the designer had come unstuck, but the fixings were slackened off, the glass was pushed back into position, and the fixings were then tightened again without difficulty. Norman Foster's ground-breaking design had proved surprisingly successful. The building has won a number of prestigious architectural awards, and in 1991 it was listed as a building of architectural interest; it is one of the youngest buildings to be Grade I listed.

Its listing meant that when the quarter-Olympic-size swimming pool was closed in the 1990s, the firm was told it could not remove it. Instead of filling in the pool, the company built a floor over the top and added to its office space in that way. A glass strip was inserted in the floor around the perimeter of the pool, so it is possible still to look down and see the now-empty pool.

Ipswich residents have now got used to the reflection of the Unitarian Meeting House and St Nicholas's Church in the walls of what they still insist on calling the Willis Faber building, and Sir Norman Foster has gone on to design other prestigious and sometimes controversial buildings.

WITCHES, IPSWICH
☛ *See Speedway, Ipswich*

WOLSEY, THOMAS
The son of Robert Wolsey, a successful Ipswich businessman, perhaps a butcher, and his wife Joan, Thomas Wolsey was almost certainly a pupil of the town's grammar school and went to Magdalen College, Oxford, when he was eleven. Ordained priest in 1498, he became a parish priest in Somerset, but he was destined for greater things. He became chaplain to the Archbishop of Canterbury in 1501, later chaplain to Henry VII, for whom he was soon engaged on diplomatic rather than spiritual missions. For fourteen years he served as Lord Chancellor to King Henry VIII, and during that period he was without doubt the most powerful man in England next to the king.

Cardinal Wolsey, a print from a well-known portrait by Hans Holbein.

As Lord Chancellor he was the king's chief minister, combining the work of the present-day foreign secretary and home secretary and much more besides. He has been much criticised for the magnificence of his household and for the style in which he lived, but magnificence was a political weapon which Wolsey wielded tirelessly on the king's behalf.

On a diplomatic mission to Francis I, King of France, in 1527 to negotiate an Anglo-French alliance Wolsey told the members of his household that they were to treat him with the respect due to the king; he was after all the king's appointed representative. His own magnificence was a statement of Henry's supremacy. The papal nuncio in France said of Wolsey that 'although in all his outward acts he shows excessive pomp and great ostentation,

'Reputed Birth-Place of Wolsey' reads the caption on this nineteenth-century photograph of the chemist's shop on the corner of Silent Street and St Nicholas Street. In fact Thomas was born in a house, long since demolished, on the other side of St Nicholas Street.

nevertheless, in speaking, in behaviour and in negotiation, he reveals an intellect capable of every greatness, proper to any undertaking or affair, because he is a dexterous and gracious man, full of glorious and noble intentions'.

At the height of his power Cardinal Wolsey made plans to found a college at Oxford with feeder schools in fifteen English dioceses, the main school being in Ipswich. Work on Cardinal College at Oxford began in 1525, and three years later he was gathering materials for the Ipswich school to be built on the site of the Priory of SS Peter & Paul, which was dissolved to provide some of the money for the project. In the opening months of 1529 the two master masons, Richard Lee and a man named Barbour, showed the plans of the proposed Ipswich college to Wolsey, who took a personal interest in its progress, and building work began. The school or college came into being before the buildings were complete and operated for a year before Wolsey fell, it was closed down and the building materials were appropriated by the king.

Wolsey died at Leicester on 29 November 1530, and was buried there in the Abbey of St Mary of the Meadows.

See S.J. Gunn & P.G. Linley, *Cardinal Wolsey: Church, state and art* (Cambridge University Press, 1991)

☛ *See also Grammar School; Silent Street; Wolsey's gate*

WOLSEY'S GATE

The only remnant of Cardinal Wolsey's college is a brick gateway in College Street immediately to the east of St Peter's Church, now showing not only its age but also the erosion caused by passing traffic. This was not the main gate but merely a small gateway for people arriving by water; in the sixteenth century the quayside was much closer than it is now. Above the gate are the Royal Arms of Henry VIII, though the brickwork is now so eroded that they are difficult to see.

WORBY, WILLIAM

When employed as foreman by the Ransomes at the Old Foundry in St Margaret's Ditches, Worby set up a branch works, which eventually grew into the Orwell Works. He later became works manager, and was closely involved with John Fowler in the development of a balance plough for use with Fowler's steam ploughing engines.

☛ *See also Orwell Works; Ransome & Co.; Ransomes, Sims & Jefferies*

WORKING MEN'S COLLEGE

Inaugurated in 1864 by an energetic parson who was keen to provide education for working people with little schooling, the Ipswich Working Men's College met in the Old Assembly Rooms in Tavern Street. In charge was the Rev. F. Barham Zincke, the vicar of Wherstead, who wrote his history of Wherstead as a series of letters to the *Suffolk Chronicle*. Members paid an annual subscription of 2s. 6d. (12½p) to attend evening classes in such subjects as arithmetic, chemistry, book-keeping and foreign languages.

☛ *See also Institute, The Ipswich*

Wolsey's Gate was in much better condition in the Edwardian era, as seen here, than it is today.

WYKES BISHOP

The Bishop's Wick, or Wicks Episcopi as it was sometimes called, was one of the four hamlets into which the town was once divided. Before the Norman Conquest it was an estate held by Queen Edith, the wife of Edward the Confessor. It is the area to the south of the Felixstowe road, part of which is now called Bishops Hill, extending to the river and including Holywells Park, where the Bishop of Norwich's residence stood within the extensive moat that is still to be seen. The site would have given the bishop a splendid view of the town and port. Wykes Bishop continued in the hands of successive bishops from 1235 until the properties of the diocese were exchanged for those of St Benet's Abbey by Henry VIII.

☛ *See also Holywells Park*

WYKES UFFORD

Two carucates of land, which before the Conquest had been held by Earl Gyrth, passed into the new king's hands in 1066 and were controlled by Roger Bigot, Sheriff of Norfolk and Suffolk. It was an area to the north-west of Bishops Hill and extending as far as Westerfield. The name derives from its having become the property of the later Ufford earls of Suffolk.